£4.95

CW01632813

SIVANANDA YOGA VEDANTA CENTRE

51 Felsham Road,

London, SW15 1AZ

Tel: 0181-780 0160

Fax: 0181-780 0128

Yoga Classes, Books and Tapes

YOGA ASANAS

YOGA ASANAS

SRI SWAMI SIVANANDA

Published By

THE DIVINE LIFE SOCIETY
P.O. SHIVANANDANAGAR—249 192
Distt. Tehri-Garhwal, U.P., Himalayas, India

Price] 1993 [Rs. 35/-

Nineteenth Edition: 1993
(6,000 Copies)

©The Divine Life Trust Society

ISBN 81-7052-008-8

Published by Swami Krishnananda for The Divine Life Society,
Shivanandanagar, and printed by him at the
Yoga-Vedanta Forest Academy Press, P.O. Shivanandanagar,
Distt. Tehri-Garhwal, U.P., Himalayas, India

PUBLISHERS' NOTE

The Yoga Asanas have acquired an importance which has a twofold character. They are not only a set of all-round physical execises but a preparatory stage for the practice of Yoga. Both the Hatha Yoga and the Raja Yoga prescribe these techniques of Asanas for the purification of the body and the setting of it in tune with the nervous equilibrium that is necessary for engaging oneself in the higher concentration. Though the Raja Yoga of Patanjali mentions any particular pose as the requisite for the practice of meditation, the Hatha Yoga lays emphasis on the practice of the different kinds of Asanas for maintaining a healthy condition of the body and also to bring about a rhythm in its functions so that this may be conducive to the still subtler process of introducing a balance and rhythm in the flow of the Pranas by the practice of Pranayama. Thus Yoga Asanas form the very foundation of Yoga proper.

The author, Sri Swami Sivanandaji Maharaj, well-known for his blending of the various Yogas as steps, stages and processes in the One Yoga of meditation on the Absolute, describes in the present volume the Yoga Asanas in a homely way so that they may be intelligible even to a layman. Highly technical descriptions have been purposely avoided to enable the common man to derive benefit from them easily and to introduce him to a realm above his usual worldly routine. Important postures are illustrated separately for practical guidance in Yoga Asana practice, though it is always advisable to learn the Asanas directly from a teacher. We have no doubt that the public and aspirants of Yoga will receive this publication with joy.

The Yoga Asana postures appended to this volume are by Brahmachari Bhubanananda Dash.

—THE DIVINE LIFE SOCIETY

DEVI STOTRA

शरणागतदीनार्तपरित्राणपरायणे।
सर्वस्यार्तिहरे देवि नारायणि नमोऽस्तु ते॥१॥

1. O Narayani! Devoted to the deliverance of the distressed, the meek and the shelter-seekers! O Devi! The destroyer of distresses of all! Be this bow to Thee.

GURU STOTRA

गुरुमूर्तिं स्मरेन्नित्यं गुरोर्नाम सदा जपेत्।
गुरोराज्ञां प्रकुर्वीत गुरोरन्यन्नभावयेत्॥२॥

2. One should always remember the form of Guru, always repeat His Name, carry out His Orders and should think of nothing else.

गुरुरेको जगत्सर्वं ब्रह्मविष्णुशिवात्मकम्।
गुरोः परतरं नास्ति तस्मात् संपूजयेद् गुरुम्॥३॥

3. The whole world representing Brahma (Creator), Vishnu (Protector) and Siva (Destroyer) is only the Guru (manifested). One should adore his Guru, as there is no one other than the Guru.

Om Santih! Om Santih! Om Santih!

PARA PUJA

The Highest Worship

O Lord Kesava, what I am thinking of is this: How am I to please Thee?

1. The Ganga itself is flowing from Thy feet, shall I take water for Thy ablution then?

2. Thou hast Sat-Chit-Ananda (Absolute Existence, Absolute Consciousness and Absolute Bliss) Svarupa (aspects) as Thy cloth. What Pitambara (yellow cloth) shall I dress Thee with?

3. Thou art dwelling in all creatures and inanimate objects of the Universe. O Vasudeva! What Asana shall I give Thee to sit on?

4. Both the Sun and the Moon are serving Thee all through; what is the use of showing Thee a looking-glass in vain?

5. Thou art the Light of all lights. Now tell me, what other light shall I burn for Thee?

6. The Anahata (unceasing eternal sound of 'Om') is being continued all day and night to welcome Thee. Shall I then play on drums and cymbals or sound a conch to please Thee?

7. All the four Vedas, in the four speeches (sounds), are singing nothing but Thy praise; what hymns shall I sing for Thee then?

8. All the Rasas (flavours) are but Thy flavour only, what other objects shall I place before Thee, then, as Thy food, O Rama?

A UNIVERSAL PRAYER

O Loving Lord, Ocean of mercy!
O Thou Infinite Sea of serenity!

Thou art Varuna, Indra, Brahma, Rudra,
Father, Mother, Grandsire of all.
Thou art the blue sky, moon and stars,
Hail, hail to Thee, a thousand times all hail!

Thou art within, without, above, below,
On every side, front, behind and all around,
Thou art Antaryamin, Witness and the Lord,
Hail unto Thee! again, all hail!

Thou art all-pervading and interpenetrating.
Thou art Sutratman, like the string of a garland.
Thou art life, intelligence, thought or consciousness.
Bless me to behold Thee everywhere and in everyone.

O Sweet Adorable Presence! the Glory of glories,
The Sun of suns, Light of lights, Deity of deities!
Remove the veil of ignorance that blurs my vision,
And grant me strength to realise my oneness with Thee.

INTRODUCTION

I bow with folded hands, crores of times, to Brahman, the destroyer of all fears, miseries and tribulations of those who betake themselves to Him, which though absolutely unborn (*Aja*) appears by the power of His greatness to pass into birth, which appears as if in motion, though always at rest (*Achala*), and which, though one, (*Ekam-eva-advitiyam Brahma*) appears as many to those whose inner vision is dimmed by the perception of an endless variety of illusory appearances.

I salute Thee, first Lord Siva (*Adinatha*), who taught to Parvati the Hatha-Vidya that is a step to the attainment of the most excellent Raja Yoga.

Goraksha and Matsyendra knew well the Hatha-Vidya. Yogi Swatmarama learnt it from them by their favour. To those who wander about in the darkness of this science or branch of Yoga unable to obtain any knowledge of Hatha Yoga, the most merciful Swatmarama Yogi offers the light of Hatha-Vidya.

The goal of life is Self-realisation. All systems of Indian philosophy have one goal in view, the liberation of the soul through perfection.

Every man wants happiness. He shuns pain. No one teaches anyone to seek happiness. It is the innate, inherent Svabhava (nature) of everyone to seek happiness. Ananda is embodiment of one's own nature.

Gratification of desires cannot bring in real peace of mind though the nerves are tickled for a second. Just as ghee when poured over the fire aggravates the fire, so also enjoyment intensifies a desire and makes the mind all the more restless. How can you expect real, lasting happiness from objects that are conditioned in time, space and causation and so are Vinasi (perishable) and Anitya (impermanent)?

The happiness that you get from sensual objects is fleeting and transitory. For a philosopher it is no happiness at all. It is like scratching the skin when you get itching. Sensual happiness is attended with severe exertion, sin, fear, pain, worry and several evils.

Amidst the din and boisterous bustle of worldly activities there come moments of tranquillity and peace when the mind, for the time being, however short it may be, soars above the filthy worldly things and reflects on the higher problems of life—viz., "Who am I? Whence? Where? Whither? Why of Universe?" etc. The sincere enquirer becomes serious and extends his reflections. He begins to search and understand the truth. Discrimination dawns on him. He takes to the study of Atma-Jnana books, reflects, meditates, purifies his mind and eventually attains the highest knowledge of the Self. But the man whose mind is saturated with worldly Vasanas and cravings is quite heedless and is irresistibly carried away by the two currents of Raga-Dvesha and tossed about helplessly in the tumultous Samsaric stream of birth and death with its concomitant evils.

The spiritual path is thorny, precipitous and nevertheless has been trodden by man of strong determination, undaunted spirit and indomitable energy. When once you make up your mind to tread the path, everything will become smooth and easy. You will have descent of Grace from the Lord. The whole spiritual world will back you up. The path will directly take you to realms of Infinite Bliss, Supreme Peace, Eternal Sunshine—realms where three kinds of Tapa, cares, worries, anxieties and fear, which torment the soul here dare not enter, where all distinctions of caste, creed and colour vanish altogether in the one embrace of Divine Love and where desires and cravings find their full satiety.

Just as one and the same coat will not suit Mr. John, Mr. Das or Mr. Pantulu, so also one path will not suit all people. There are four paths to suit people of four kinds of temperament. They all lead to the same goal, the attainment of ultimate Reality. Roads are different but the destination is the same. The four paths that are inculcated for the achievement of this ultimate Truth from the different stand-points of the man of action, the man of devotion, the mystic man and the philosopher or the man of reason, are respectively termed Karma Yoga, Bhakti Yoga, Raja Yoga and Jnana Yoga.

The four paths are not antagonistic to one another, but, on the other hand, they are complementary. They only indicate that the different methods of the Hindu religion are in harmony with each other. Religion must educate and develop the whole man, his heart, intellect (head) and hand. Then only will he reach perfection. One-sided development is not commendable. Karma Yoga removes Mala, purifies the mind and develops the hand. Bhakti Yoga destroys Vikshepa and develops the heart. Raja Yoga steadies the mind and makes it one-pointed. Jnana Yoga removes the veil of ignorance (Avarana), develops will and reason and brings in knowledge of the Self. Therefore one should practise the four Yogas. You can have Jnana Yoga as the centre and the other Yogas as auxiliaries to get rapid progress in the spiritual path.

The word 'Yoga' means union between Jivatma and Paramatma (individual soul and Supreme Soul). The science that teaches the way of acquiring this occult knowledge is called Yoga Sastra. Hatha Yoga concerns with the physical body and control of breath. Raja Yoga deals with the mind. Raja Yoga and Hatha Yoga are necessary counterparts of each other. No one can become a perfect Yogi without a knowledge of the practices of both. Raja Yoga begins where properly practised Hatha Yoga ends.

Hatha is considered to be a compound word formed of two syllables 'Ha' and 'tha'; 'Ha' means the moon (Ida Nadi) and 'tha' means the sun (Pingala). These correspond to the breaths, which flow through the left and right nostrils. Hatha Yoga teaches the way to unite the sun and the moon, the Prana and Apana through the regulation of breath.

Hatha Yoga is conducive to health and longevity. Its practice regulates the action of heart, lungs and brain. It promotes digestion and circulation of blood. Kidneys, liver and all other internal viscera work efficiently. It removes all sorts of diseases.

This book 'YOGA ASANAS' deals with 90 poses of the body with important Bandhas and Mudras and system of Pranayamas, prescribed by the Yoga Sastras. Pranayama goes hand in hand with Asanas. The first two accessories of Yoga are Yama and Niyama. Asana is the third Anga of Ashtanga Yoga, while Pranayama is the fourth Anga. The wise Rishis of yore had formulated these as aids to spiritual culture and preservation of a high standard of health, vigour and vitality.

Ordinary physical exercises develop the superficial muscles of the body only. One can become a Sandow with a beautiful physique. But Asanas are intended for the thorough exercise of the internal organs, viz., liver, spleen, pancreas, intestines, heart, lungs, brain and the important ductless glands of the body which are called endocrine glands, viz., thyroid and parathyroid at the root of the neck, adrenals in spleen, pituitary and pineal glands in brain which play a very important part in the economy of nature, in maintaining health in metabolism and in structure, growth and nutrition of different kinds of cells and tissues of the body.

Detailed instructions regarding the technique of the poses and their illustrations are given in this book so that anyone can practise them easily even by a perusal of it.

India today is in need of a strong and healthy race of men. Various factors have brought about their degeneration. Regular and judicious practice of these valuable exercises prescribed by our Rishis of yore will doubtless pave a long way in regenerating the race and in the production of such a strong and healthy race.

"*Sthira-sukham asanam*—Posture is that which is firm and comfortable." It should not cause any painful sensation or trouble. If the Asanas are not firm, the mind will be disturbed quickly. You will not have concentration of mind. The body must be firm as the rock. There must not be the least shaking of the body. If the seat becomes firm, you will have progress in your meditation. You will have no consciousness of the body.

In olden days these Asanas were practised in Gurukulas and so the people were strong and healthy and had long life. In schools and colleges these Asanas should be introduced.

The postures are as many in numbers as there are numbers of species of living creatures in this Universe (84 lacs of bodies). There are 84 lacs of Asanas described by Lord Siva. Among them 84 are the best and among these 84, 32 have been found very useful for mankind.

Man has reached his present state after passing through 84 lacs of Yonis (different wombs). A thorough critical study of the human wombs will reveal traces of all different incarnations of the past.

There are some Asanas which can be practised while standing. They are Tadasana, Trikonasana, Garudasana, etc. There are some which can be practised sitting. They are Paschimottanasana, Janusirshasana, Padmasana, Lolasana, etc. Some are practised while lying down. These are Utthanapádasana, Pavanamuktasana. Weak and delicate persons can do Asanas while lying down. Some Asanas such as Sirshasana, Vrikshasana, Sarvangasana, Viparita Karani

Mudra, etc., are done with head downwards and legs upwards.

Generally after the age of ten or twelve these Asanas can be practised. People of twenty or thirty years of age perform all Asanas nicely. Practice for a month or two will render all rigid tendons, muscles and bones very elastic. Even old persons can practise all Asanas. They can give up Sirshasana if they are not physically fit. There are persons of advanced age who practise Sirshasana also.

A Vedantin is afraid to do Asanas and Pranayamas on the ground that the practice will intensify Dehadhyasa and militate against his practice of Vairagya. Though the two paths Hatha Yoga and Vedanta are entirely different yet a Vedantin can harmoniously combine Pranayamas and Asanas to his best advantage. I have seen many Vedantins in a sickly condition with very poor physique and dilapidated constitution. They can hardly do any kind of intense Vedantic Sadhana. They may utter "Om, Om, Om," mechanically through lips only. They have not got the strength inside to raise the proper Brahmakara-Vritti from the pure Sattvic Antahkarana. The body is closely related to the mind. A weak, sickly body means a weak mind also. If the Vedantin does a little practice of Pranayama and Asanas to keep up his body and mind strong and healthy, he can do very good Nididhyasana and turn out efficient spiritual work. Though the body is Jada (insentient) and useless, yet it is an important instrument for Self-realisation. The instrument must be kept clean, strong and healthy. This body is a horse for you to take you to the goal. If the horse tumbles down you cannot reach the destination. If this instrument breaks down, you will not reach the goal of "Atma-Sakshatkara."

The purification is acquired by the regular performance of six practices (Shat Karmas), viz., (1) Dhauti, (2) Basti, (3) Neti, (4) Nauli, (5) Trataka and (6) Kapalabhati.

Asana or posture gives strength. Mudra gives steadiness (Sthirata). Pratyahara gives calmness (Dhairya). Pranayama produces lightness of body. Dhyana gives perception (Pratyakshatva) of Self. Samadhi gives isolation (Nirliptata) or Kaivalyam which is verily the freedom or final beatitude.

Since the dawn of history, various extraordinary phenomena have been regarded as happening amongst human beings. In the West the experiences of many religious persons have been recorded under the heading "Cosmic Consciousness." Expert Occultists demonstrated the phenomenon of separating the astral body from the physical body. Some surface scientists, if unable to explain the various extraordinary Yogic phenomena, try to ignore them. Many sensible scientists are endeavouring to study, investigate and generalise such extraordinary phenomena, which are the outcome of rigid Yogic practices. Man can control his inner and outer nature and transmute himself into Divinity.

Late Trailinga Swami of Varanasi, Jnanadeva of Alandi, Raja Bhartrihari, Chang Dev had all raised themselves to Godhead through Yogic Sadhana. What one has attained can be achieved by every one of us, if we earnestly strive to get at it. It is a question of supply and demand. The supply will come at once, if there will be a keen demand for the same. The question is: "Do you demand God? Are you spiritually thirsty and hungry?"

May Joy, Bliss, Immortality, Peace, Poise, Glory and Splendour abide in you all for ever!

GOOD VISION

Lost in the never-ending and ever-increasing distractions and sensual excitement of modern living, man is abusing his senses far beyond their normal capacity and then complaining that they begin to lose their efficiency long before the normal fading out of old age.

To satisfy the jaded palate, hotter and hotter, sweeter and sweeter, saltier and saltier or sourer and sourer condiments are added to his food—long since have the original tastes of vegetables, fruits and cereals been lost and forgotten, never to be recaptured by his coarsened tongue.

The scent of the rose or the ripening corn, the perfumes wafted by a cool evening breeze—all are lost to the nose now adapted to petrol fumes. The stench of duco-spraying and the suffocating atmosphere of entertainment-halls.

But surely the most abused of man's senses is sight as, from the days when he first invented the printing of black letters on dazzling white paper and took to reading this print under artificial light, extending his open-eyed period by a third to half a day and, under the cruel stress of competitive examinations, even to two-thirds of a day, he enjoys normal vision for a mere fraction of his life-span and frequently becomes a 'four-eyed' long before leaving school. The pleasure of walking after dark unaided by torch or street-light, using instead eyes, ears and nose, is unbelievable to this 'civilised' man who would rather fill his pre-slumber hours staring at a rectangle of flickering pictures, for the last forty or fifty years in the cinema hall, but now more temptingly in the television of his own home.

Man cannot renew his organs of sense but, once convinced of the futility of their further abuse and inevitable weakening, he can reduce unnatural living habits and begin to recover a little of their intended power, flexibility and usefulness by exercising lazy muscles.

Most eye-fatigue is due to the eyes being held for long periods at the one focus, that of reading, relieved occasionally by glancing about the room or a few feet ahead while walking. Break this wearing habit by, at every excuse, getting outdoors and gazing into the distance. Try to revitalise those eye muscles, day by day, seeing the horizon more clearly. Look at the clouds but not directly at the sun.

Trataka or sun-gazing has developed a bad reputation due to its ignorant practice. If the sun's rays are allowed to penetrate the unprotected eye by Trataka, done with the sun in the high heavens, great damage is done and permanent blindness may result. A little Trataka when the sun has just risen above the flat horizon—not hours later when it rises above the high hills—will help to cleanse the eye and increase concentration but, if at all, do it with caution!

The following simple exercises have improved eyesight to the extent of allowing some people to again read a newspaper without glasses, depending of course on the nature of the eye-weakness.

EXERCISE I: Focus intently on a distant object—for a normal-sighted man on the horizon but for the weak-sighted on the farthest object you can see clearly, day by day coaxing the eyes to see further—then, without moving the eyes, straighten out an arm in front of you and lift the forefinger to cover the distant object. You will see the original object plus two fingers, because the finger is out of focus.

Now stare at the finger, then at the distant object. Repeat five or six times.

Focussing on the finger-tip slowly move the finger towards the eyes till it rests on the forehead between the eyebrows. Now the eyes are closed. Hold them thus until you feel a slight strain, then slowly straighten the arm, returning the finger to its original position before the distant object. As soon as the finger leaves the forehead concentrate again on the finger-tip. When the arm straightens focus on the distant object, then on the finger-tip and repeat several times.

EXERCISE II: Repeat the above exercise but bring the finger, eyes focussed on its tip, slowly to the end of the nose.

While doing these eye-movements try to remain unblinking, eyes open continuously, thus practising a form of Trataka and improving your concentration and one-pointedness of mind.

EXERCISE III: Without moving the head, turn the eyes to look as far as possible first to the left, then slowly the diagonals, starting with the top left corner, slowly down to the right, up to the sky, down to the ground; then along to the bottom right corner, to bottom left corner and finishing at top right corner.

EXERCISE IV: (This exercise will help concentration because you must think simultaneously of both your breathing and movement of the eyes.) Look down to the ground. Then slowly make a big circle to the left, above, to the right and down again with the eyes, breathing in deeply and trying to have capacity breath when the eye-circle is completed. Repeat the slow circling to the left, this time breathing out to empty the lungs as the circle is completed. Repeat both sequences to the right. The circles must be as large as possible.

EXERCISES V, VI: There are endless shapes—letters of the alphabet, the square, the diamond, the figure eight, firstly upright and then lying on its side—which can be drawn with the eyes.

Practise these exercises sincerely in the open air but not in direct sunlight. Each time as you finish cover the eyes with the palms of the hands, open them in the dark and breathe deeply, concentrating intently on the open eyes especially as you breathe out, thus sending plenty of Pranic energy along with fresh blood-supply to the eyes. Close the eyes again before removing the hands to avoid sudden glare. You can do the breathing three times.

Always do your reading in a good steady light, coming from over the left shoulder and neither too bright nor too dull; do not waste your eyesight on poor, low-class cinema-shows; try to do your eyework in the natural daylight, sleeping, discussing, meditating and doing your other spiritual practices at night; live as much as possible in nature, letting the eyes rest on its greens and blues. The green of trees and hills is your eyes' best tonic.

May you have speedy good-vision through leading a simple, healthy and inspiring life, seeing all as good and perfect.

—SWAMI KARUNANANDA

FLEXIBILITY

The grasses bow before the gale and again raise their heads to the midday sun. The proud giants above remain stiff, not budging an inch, only to be rudely uprooted.

The humble servant prostrates to all and goes on serving till retired by old age while his unbending master is envied, deposed and disposed of in his prime.

"Truly a flexible back makes for a long life."

(Chinese Proverb)

Also for a spiritual aspirant mental flexibility is necessary. Great civilisations have come and gone, sometimes, as with Atlantis, leaving little or no trace for the curious historians, often due to rigidity of ideas—an inability to adapt to changing conditions—whereas Hindu culture, surely the world's oldest unbroken tradition, lives on and flourishes because it modifies itself and becomes richer with the changing pattern of history.

In the individual, mental and physical flexibility go together. Physical flexibility and discipline are necessary for successful concentration and development of mental power. The great Rishis and Yogis of our timeless heritage gained their incomparable spiritual insight only after Tapasya or physical disciplines, which freed the body from the pangs of hunger and thirst, heat and cold. Complete freedom, resulting in remarkable agility of mind and body, comes only after a long, severe self-disciplining.

From time immemorial a part of the physical disciplining has been the regular and devoted practice of Yoga Asanas and Pranayama, performed reverently and selflessly even to the day of discarding one's earthly body. Such practice helps greatly in the act of dying also. How blessed is the man who leaves his body while meditating in the All-pervading One!

O Seeker! Make Asanas and Pranayama part of your daily devotional offering to God, doing them whole-heartedly and with the utmost perfection of which you are capable. Your aim should be to do them more perfectly from day to day, always knowing that real perfection moves on before you, ever leading you on but never to be captured.

To increase your mastery over Asanas start daily with flexibility exercises, mostly based on the largest possible circular movement at the main joints of the body, beginning with:

I. Neck (can be done seated or standing).

(1) With neck relaxed drop head back as far as possible. Hold for a few seconds, then slowly lift head. Let it drop forward till chin touches chest at hollow at the base of throat. Hold for a few seconds.

(2) With head upright and shoulders steady, turn head slowly to look as far as possible over left shoulder. Hold for a few seconds, then slowly turn head to look as far as possible over right shoulder. Hold for a few seconds, then slowly face front.

(3) With head facing front and neck relaxed, drop head towards left shoulder as far as possible. Hold for a few seconds, then slowly lift head. Let it drop towards right shoulder as far as possible. Hold for a few seconds then.

(4) Begin slowly to circle head on completely relaxed neck, three times in each direction.

II. Shoulder circling (can be done seated or standing).

(1) Circle as large as possible with left shoulder only, forward, down, back and up, three times. Repeat with right shoulder. Then moving both shoulders together.

(2) As (1) above but circle in reverse, back, down, forward and up.

(3) Raise left shoulder as far as possible. Hold for a few seconds, then drop. Repeat three times. Repeat with right shoulder. Repeat with both shoulders together. All the following exercises are done standing.

III. Arm circling with concentration on shoulder-joint. Arm straight but relaxed.

(1) Make a smooth circle as large as possible with left arm, three times—back and up breathing in, forward and down breathing out. Repeat with right arm.

(2) As (1) but forward and up breathing in, back and down and stretch three times. Reverse.

(3) Make a smooth circle as large as possible with both arms moving to the sides and crossing above the head, breathing in. Then continue circling of arms across body on the way down, breathing out. Repeat three times.

(4) As (3) but begin crossing arms in front of body on way up, breathing in deeply till arms part above head, then breathe out as arms come down to sides of body.

IV. Lower arm circling with concentration on elbow-joint and with upper arm steady. Being with arms stretched to sides, then bend at elbows, moving lower arms up, down and stretched three times. Reverse.

V. Hand circling with concentration on wrist, arms stretched to sides.

(1) Forward, down, back and up three times, then

(2) Reverse.

(3) Lift hand as far as possible, not moving the rest of arm. Let hand drop. Repeat three times.

VI. For flexibility of knuckles stretch arms fully to sides, then relax at knuckles, letting fingers drop. Stretch fingers and drop, three times.

VII. With arms stretched to sides clench fists tightly, then stretch fingers. Repeat three times.

VIII. Stretch arms to sides, then relax at elbow and wrist, letting arms bend. Stretch and relax three times.

Finish by stretching arms to sides as far as possible. Hold for a few seconds, then let arms drop.

IX. To stretch and strenghthen muscles of arms, shoulders, chest and back, raise arms to side as you breathe in deeply, then clench hooked fingers in front of body with arms parallel to ground. Hold breath and pull hard as though to pull fingers apart. Hold for a few seconds then let arms drop and relax. Once only.

X. Hands pressed together as in Indian salutation but with arms stretched above the head. Breathe deeply and hold breath. Press hands hard then slowly bring arms down, keeping fingers pointing upwards, until at about waist level hands start to part. Flick them apart suddenly breathing out. Once only.

XI. Hands pressed together as in Indian salutation but with arms behind the back. Slowly work the hands as far as possible up the spine. Then press them together hard and pull them down the spine, keeping fingers pointing upwards, until at about waist level hands start to part. Flick them apart suddenly, breathing out. Once only.

XII. Bring left arm up the back as far as possible. At the same time bring right arm over right shoulder till you can clench fingers of both hands behind back. Breathe deeply, hold breath and pull. Hold for a few seconds, then relax. Once only. Repeat over left shoulder.

XIII. Nauli Kriya. For flexibility of stomach muscles and ideal for constipation. Can be divided into four stages.

(1) Uddiyana Bandha. Exhale fully, bend forward to expel air from lungs. Straighten body without breathing in, but lifting chest. Hold for a few seconds. This pulls abdomen back and up and massages digestive and excretory organs.

(2) As (1) then with knees slightly bent, press hands on thighs and try to bring forward the central muscles of the belly, rectus abdominus muscles, to stand out as a column.

All but fat people can do (1) but (2), (3) and (4) need patient practice.

(3) As (2) but pressing with one hand only, so bringing one muscle forward at a time.

(4) Alternate the pressure on thighs thus creating circular movement with muscles. This is Nauli Kriya.

Exercises (2), (3) and (4) can be done three or four times each.

XIV. For flexibility of hips and lower spine.

(1) Stand erect, heels together. Relax by bending left leg and putting weight of body on straight leg. Keep heels flat on ground. Pelvis slopes down from right to left. Reverse position of legs. Pelvis slopes down from left to right. Repeat five or six times, gradually increasing speed. Concentrate on movement of pelvis.

(2) Stand erect, heels together. Bend slightly at knees. Keeping rest of body steady, tip pelvis backward and forward as far as possible. Due to stiffness of lower spine at first little or no movement may be possible.

(3) Bend slightly at knees as in (2). Make small, smooth circle of hips, connecting movements (1) and (2). Three times clockwise and anticlockwise.

(4) Stand erect, heels together. Push lower spine and pelvis over to left as far as possible, retaining balance with head directly above feet, i.e., body arched to left. Outside leg straight, inner leg bent. Bend both legs, pushing lower spine and pelvis across to right as far as possible. Repeat to left and right three times.

(5) Stand erect, heels together. Push belly forward as far as possible, i.e., whole of body arched to front with head remaining directly above feet. Bending legs, push lower spine and pelvis back as far as possible till legs are straight and upper body bent forward, with arms hanging vertically. Again bend legs and push lower spine and pelvis forward through the hanging arms till the body is again arched forward. Repeat three times.

(6) Make circle as large as possible connecting movements of (4) and (5) pushing hard in each direction. Three times clockwise and anticlockwise.

(7) Stand erect, heels together. Without moving legs, push trunk as far as possible to left, feeling stretch at right side of waist, contraction at left. Reverse. Repeat three times.

(8) Arching body forward bend back as far as possible, letting head drop back relaxed and arms hang to sides, legs bent. Hold for a few seconds, then slowly straighten up and bend forward with straight legs, trying to palce palms of hands on ground. Slowly straighten up. Repeat three times.

XV. Combination exercise for concentration and flexibility. Stand erect, heels together. Keep left arm hanging straight down at side of left leg, with fingers touching leg and sliding up and down leg during movements of rest of body. Start to make a large circle sideways, raising right arm and keeping eyes fixed on right hand. Breathe in as arm is raised. As arm reaches above head start to bend body to left. When body cannot move further to left side drop forward, breathing out, completing circle with right arm, hand touching ground in front of body. Immediately start lifting right arm and the body to right side, breathing in. Continue till body is straight, then, let arm continue upwards on second circle. Repeat three times, then reverse. Concentrate on breathing and movement at waist.

XVI. To twist spine, stretch muscles behind the legs and increase flexibility at waist.

(1) Feet well apart, legs straight, arms stretched out at sides for whole exercise. Breathe in. Keeping head and body erect, turn as far as possible to left at waist (till you can see behind you), then breathe out as you bend to left without changing arms, touching ground with right fingers behind left foot and with vertical line through arms. Breathing in, straighten till arms are again parallel with ground. Hold breath as you turn as far as possible to right at waist

(till you can see behind you). Then repeat as above to right. Do three times to both sides, then return to front and lower arms.

(2) Feet well apart and legs straight for whole exercise. Breathe in. Keeping head and body erect, turn to left at waist till head is over left leg. Bend body over left leg, breathing out, keeping legs straight and sliding hands down left leg till they touch ground. Straighten up, breathing in and still facing over left leg. Hold breath and turn to right at waist till head is over right leg. Then repeat as above to right. Do three times to both sides.

XVII. To stretch muscles and tendons on inner side of thighs and behind legs and for flexibility of spine. Slide feet apart as far as possible to sides, with body upright. Legs straight throughout exercise. Bend forward to place palms of hands on ground in front of and close to body. Bend arms and put whole forearm on ground. Put top of head on ground. Hold for a few seconds. Lift head. Straighten arms, leaving palms of hands on ground. Gradually work feet closer till heels touch with legs straight, arms straight and hands on ground. Hold for a few seconds. Straighten. Breathing normal. Concentrate on back of legs and inner side of thighs. Once only.

XVIII. For balance and to increase flexibility at hip joints. Feet well apart and arms raised to sides for whole exercise. Straighten legs, then lunge to left bending left knee and raising heel from ground, right leg stretched to side, with body as upright as possible. Keeping body low and upright, move slowly over to right side, bending right knee and raising heel from ground, left leg stretched to side. Repeat three times to both sides, then return to first position. Breathing normal. Concentrate on hip joints.

XIX. Balance and flexibility at hips.

(1) Stand erect, heels together. Keeping rest of body still, swing left leg back and forward, completely relaxed and

gradually getting higher. Height is not as important as stillness of rest of body. Four or five times each leg.

(2) As (1) but swing left leg out to left side and let it fall again. Repeat with right. Four or five times each leg.

XX. For maximum flexibility at hip-joint.

(1) Stand erect, feet together. Lift left leg to front, knee bent, till thigh is horizontal. Open leg out to left as far as possible, concentrating on hip-joint. Lower leg. Repeat three times. Then repeat with right leg.

(2) Reverse of (1). Begin by lifting left leg as far as possible to side till thigh is horizontal. Then close leg to front, concentrating on hip-joint. Lower leg to front. Repeat as (1).

XXI. Lower leg circling with concentration on knee, left leg stretched to the front upper leg kept still. Circling in, out and stretch, three times; then reverse. Repeat with right leg.

Exercises XXII, XXIII and XXIV to be completed first with left foot, then repeated three times with right foot.

XXII. Foot circling with concentration on the ankle, left leg stretched to front. Movement at ankle only. Circling in, out and stretch, three times; then reverse.

XXIII. Up and down movement of foot as far as possible, with concentration on the ankle, left leg stretched to front. Movement at ankle only, three times.

XXIV. Toe clenching and stretching, alternating with big toe on top, big toe underneath. Repeat three times.

Thus the joints have been loosened and the whole body put into a flexible condition for your Yogasana practice. When the sequence has been learned, all these exercises can be done sincerely within twenty to thirty minutes. Most can be done easily by the householder and will suffice with a little Pranayama, till such time as he can slowly add some extra Asanas.

May God bless you with health and contentment.

—SWAMI KARUNANANDA.

CONTENTS

Section Four
MISCELLANEOUS ASANAS

SECTION FIVE
IMPORTANT MUDRAS AND BANDHAS

Yoga Asanas

SECTION ONE

SURYA NAMASKARA

In the system of 'Suryanamaskara' are combined several Yoga postures with rhythmic breathing, rapid movement, sunbathing and prayerful contemplation of the divine power that the sun represents. We are asked to practise this Suryanamaskara facing the morning sun, bathing our whole body in the life-giving rays of the sun, the giver of light, life, joy and warmth to the whole world.

Suryanamaskara consists of twelve postures or stages. One posture smoothly and gracefully, flows into the next. There is fairly vigorous movement which builds up the muscles too, yet it conforms to the vitally important rule in Yoga that there should be no undue strain or violence to the practice. Hence, the extraordinary and unique result: after the practice, one does not feel tired and exhausted as it often happens in mere physical culture, but one feels thoroughly refreshed.

Of still greater importance is the inner mood with which Suryanamaskara is done. Inwardly watch every little movement, becoming aware of every change that takes place in the body, especially the spine. The mind must be quiet and observant to do this, and after a few months of practice, this awareness will grow.

TECHNIQUE

1. Stand upright. Fold the palms in front of the chest, as in the oriental way of greeting. Exhale.

2. Inhaling all the way, swing your arms up above your head, bending the trunk from the base gradually up the vertebrae as far back as you can. (Exhaling if begun

towards the end of this movement, will enable you to bend a little more).

3. Extend upwards and then forward stretching the spine and breathing out. Without bending your knees, place the palms of your hands squarely on the ground, fingers pointing straight in front, parallel to the feet. Bury the face between the knees.

4. Throw the right leg back, while inhaling. Flex the left leg at the knee and let the thigh be in close contact with the torso. Look up. Inhale.

5. Throw the left leg also back. Straighten the back and the arms. Breathe out.

6. As you breathe out, flex at the elbows. Dip the whole body and touch the ground with your forehead, chest, palms, knees and toes. The other parts of the body should not touch the ground. Keep the 'tail' up, giving a pelvic tilt.

7. Swing the head up and backwards, straighten the arms and bending the spine backwards as much as possible. Inhale.

8. As you breathe out, swing the hip up and back and assume the inverted V position, the feet and palms resting on the floor.

9. Bring the right leg forward, foot flat on floor between the hands (as 4 above). Inhale.

10. Bring the left leg forward, straighten knees, head down (as 3 above). Exhale.

11. Inhale, straighten the body, and swing your arms up above your head, bending back as far as possible (as 2 above).

12. Stand upright (as 1 above). Now resume the normal standing position. Repeat this at least twelve times every morning, alternating legs.

After completing twelve Namaskaras lie down flat on

the ground on your back and relax each and every limb one by one from toes to the crown of the head. This is called Savasana (corpse pose). To begin with if one feels tired after three or four Namaskaras he may stop with that and increase the number gradually (one everyday or every two days) all the time taking care that too much strain is not caused on any account, on any part of the body. The number should be increased according to each one's capacity. There are people, who can do 108 Namaskaras at a stretch without great strain.

Before doing the Surya-Namaskara the student may chant the prayer to the Almighty Lord:

PRAYER TO THE SUN

"Om Suryam Sundaralokanathamamritam Vedantasaram Sivam,
Jnanam Brahmamayam Suresamamalam Lokaikachittam Svayam;
Indradityanaradhipam Suragurum Trailokyachudamanim,
Brahmavishnusivasvarupahridayam Vande Sada Bhaskaram."

MEANING

I always adore Surya, the sun, the beautiful Lord of the world, the immortal, the quintessence of the Vedanta, the auspicious, the absolute knowledge, of the form of Brahman, the Lord of the gods, ever-pure, the one true consciousness of the world itself, the Lord of Indra, the gods and men, the preceptor of the gods, the crest-jewel of the three worlds, the very heart of the forms of Brahma, Vishnu and Siva, the giver of light.

The Sun being the most effulgent and life-giving force for this planet, it forms the visible representation of the invisible Almighty Lord. The vast majority of men cannot think of the transcendent Supreme Absolute without the help of some concrete object or idea. To them the Sun forms the best object for worship and meditation.

Thus, Surya-Namaskara provides the foundation for

the magnificient all-round culture of body, mind and spirit, which is essential for every human being.

SECTION TWO

ASANAS FOR DHYANA

GENERAL INSTRUCTIONS

Four Asanas are prescribed for the purposes of Japa and meditation. They are Padma, Siddha, Svastika and Sukha.

You must be able to sit in any one of these four Asanas at a stretch for full three hours without shaking the body. Then only will you get mastery over the Asana (Asana Jaya). Then only can you take to the practice of Pranayama (control of breath) and Dhyana (meditation). Without securing a steady Asana you cannot further get on well in meditation. The more steady you are in your Asana the more you will be able to concentrate and make your mind one-pointed. If you can be steady in the posture even for one hour, you will be able to acquire one-pointed mind and feel thereby infinite peace and Atmic Ananda inside.

When you sit on the posture, think: "I am as firm as a rock. Nothing can shake me." Give these suggestions to the mind a dozen times. Then the Asana will become steady soon. You must become as a living statue when you sit for Dhyana. Then only there will be real steadiness in your Asana. In one year by regular practice you will have success and you will be able to sit for three hours at a stretch. Start with half an hour and gradually increase the period.

If there is severe pain in the legs after some time, unlock the legs and then shampoo them for five minutes and sit again in the Asana. When you advance you will not experience any pain. You will experience on the other hand immense joy. Practise the Asana both morning and evening.

After sitting in the Asana close eyes and concentrate on the Bhrukuti or Trikuti (the space between the two eyebrows) or in the Anahata Chakra (lotus of the heart). As the Trikuti (Ajna Chakra) is the seat of the mind, the mind can be quite easily controlled if you concentrate gently on this spot. Ekagrata (one-pointedness of the mind) supervenes quite readily. Concentration at the tip of the nose (Nasikagra Drishti), also has the same advantage, but it takes more time for the focussing of the mind. Those who cannot concentrate either at Bhrukuti or the tip of the nose may concentrate at any other outer point or inner Chakra of heart, head, neck, etc. Gazing at Trikuti (Ajna Chakra) is also called Bhrumadhya Drishti.

Keep the head, neck and trunk in one straight line. Stick to one Asana; either Padma, Siddha, Svastika or Sukha and make it quite steady and perfect by repeated attempts. Never change the Asana. Adhere to one tenaciously. Cling to it like a leech. Realise the full benefits of one Asana for meditation.

1. PADMAṢANA

Padma means Lotus. When the Asana is demonstrated, it presents the appearance of a Lotus, in a way. Hence the name Padmasana. This is also known by the name Kamalasana.

Amongst the four poses prescribed for Japa and Dhyana, Padmasana comes foremost. It is the best Asana for contemplation. Rishis like Gheranda, Sandilya and others speak very highly of this vital Asana. This is highly agreeable for householders. Even ladies can sit in this Asana. Padmasana is suitable for lean persons and for youths as well.

TECHNIQUE

Sit on the ground by spreading the legs forward. Then

place the right foot on the left thigh and the left foot on the right thigh. Place the hands on the knee-joints.

You can make a finger-lock and keep the locked hands over the left ankle. This is very convenient for some persons. Or you can place the left hand over the left knee and then place the right hand over the right knee with the palm facing upwards and the index-finger touching the middle portion of the thumb (Chinmudra).

VARIATIONS

I. Ardha-Padmasana:

If you cannot place both the feet on the thighs at the very start, just keep one foot on one thigh for some time and the other foot on the other thigh for some time. After a few days' practice, you will be able to keep both the feet on the thighs. This is half pose of Padmasana or Ardha-Padmasana.

II. Virasana:

Sit at ease. Place the right foot on the left thigh and the left foot underneath the right thigh. Lord Gauranga used to sit on this Asana for his meditation. This is a comfortable posture. Virasana means hero posture.

III. Parvatasana (Mountain Pose):

Do ordinary Padmasana. Stand on the knees and raise your hands above. This is Parvatasana. Keep a thick blanket on the ground and then do this Asana so that you will not injure your knees. In the beginning, for a few days, catch hold of a stool or bench till you get the balance. Afterwards you can raise the hands above.

Sit on Virasana and then raise the hands above and be steady. Some persons call this also as Parvatasana.

IV. Samasana (Equal Pose):

Place the left heel at the beginning of the right thigh and the right heel at the beginning of the left thigh. Sit at ease. Do not bend either on the left or right. This is called Samasana.

V. Karmukasana:

Sit on ordinary Padmasana. Catch hold of the right toe with the right hand and the left toe with the left hand, thus making a cross of your hand at the elbow.

VI. Utthita Padmasana:

Sit on Padmasana. Keep your palms on the ground by your sides. Slowly raise the body. There should be no jerks. The body should not be trembling. Retain the breath as long as you remain in that raised position. When you come down you can exhale. Persons who cannot perform Kukkutasana can do this. The hands are kept by the sides in this Asana, but the hands are kept between the thigh and calf muscles in Kukkutasana. This is the difference.

VII. Baddha Padmasana:

Some people call this pose Padmasana.

VIII. Urdhva Padmasana

IX. Lolasana

X. Kukkutasana

XI. Tolangulasana

2. SIDDHASANA

Next to Padmasana comes Siddhasana in importance. Some eulogise this Asana as even superior to Padmasana for the purpose of Dhyana (contemplation). If you get mastery over this Asana, you will acquire many Siddhis (powers). Further it was practised by many Siddhas (perfect Yogins) of yore. Hence the name Siddhasana.

Even fat persons with big thighs can practise this Asana easily. In fact, this is better to some persons than Padmasana. Young Brahmacharins who attempt to get established in celibacy should practise this Asana. This is not suitable for ladies.

TECHNIQUE

Place one heel at the anus (Guda), the terminal opening of the alimentary canal or digestive tube. Keep the other heel at the root of the generative organ. The feet or legs should be so nicely arranged that the ankle-joints should touch each other. Hands can be placed as shown in Padmasana.

VARIATIONS

I. Guptasana (Hidden Pose):

The left heel is placed over the organ of generation. The right heel is also over the externel organ of generation. The two ankles are in close apposition or contact. The right toes are thrust inside the hollow between the left thigh and left calf muscles. The left toes are covered by the right leg. Gupta means hidden. As this Asana hides well the organ of generation it is called Guptasana.

II. Vajrasana (Adamantine Pose):

The left heel is placed below the organ of generation. The right heel is placed over the organ. Vajra means adamantine. There is also another variety of Vajrasana. Instructions are given elsewhere.

III. Baddhayonyasana:

Sit on ordinary Siddhasana and do Yoni Mudra. It is called Baddhayonyasana. The description of Yoni Mudra is given along with other Mudras.

IV. Kshemasana:

By sitting on Siddhasana if you raise your hands together up to your chest level, it is called Kshemasana. It is meant that you are praying for the Kshema (welfare) of the public. The palms must be facing each other.

V. Sthirasana (Firm Pose):

Some people call the ordinary Siddhasana as Sthirasana.

VI. Muktasana:

Ordinary Siddhasana is known as Muktasana also.

3. SVASTIKASANA

Svastikasana is sitting at ease with the body erect. Spread the legs forward. Fold the left leg and place the feet near the right thigh muscles. Similarly, bend the right leg and push it in the space between the left thigh and calf muscles. Now you will find the two feet between the thighs and calves of the legs. This is very comfortable for meditation. Keep the hands as instructed in Padmasana.

4. SUKHASANA

Any easy comfortable posture for Japa and meditation is Sukhasana, the important point being the head, neck and trunk should be in a line without curve. People who begin Japa and meditation after 30 or 40 years of age, generally are not able to sit in Padma, Siddha, or Svastikasana for a long time. I will describe now a nice form of Sukhasana in which old persons can sit and meditate for a long time. This specially suits old people who are unable to sit in Padma or Siddhasana in spite of repeated attempts. Young people also can practise this.

TECHNIQUE

Take a cloth 5 cubits long. Fold it nicely lengthwise till the width becomes half a cubit. Sit in your usual way keeping the feet below your thighs. Raise the two knees above to the level of your chest till you get a space of 8 or 10 inches between the two knees. Now take the folded cloth. Keep one end near the left knee; going to the back by the left side, touching the right knee, come to the starting point and make a knot of the two ends. Keep your palms face to face and place them between the knees. In this Asana the hands, legs and backbone are supported. Hence you will never feel tired. If you cannot do any other Asanas, sit at least in this Asana and do Japa and meditation for a long time.

VARIATIONS

I. Pavanamuktasana:

Sit down and keep the heels together and knees raised to the chest level. Bind the knees with two hands.

II. Vama Pavanamuktasana:

Here the right knee only is raised from the ground. It is bound by the two hands as in Pavanamuktasana.

III. Dakshina Pavanamuktasana:

In this posture the right knee is raised and bound by the hands and the left leg is kept on the ground.

The above three Asanas can be done when you are lying on the ground.

IV. Bhairavasana:

Sit in Vama Pavanamuktasana. Instead of binding the two knees with the hands, just keep the hands near the foot by the side of the thighs.

BENEFITS OF PADMA, SIDDHA, AND SVASTIKA ASANAS

Books on Hatha Yoga eulogise the merits and advantages of Padma and Siddhasanas to a very high degree. He who sits in any one of the Asanas even for 15 minutes daily with closed eyes, concentrating on God at the lotus of the heart, destroys all sins and gets Moksha quickly. These Asanas increase digestive fire and give good appetite, health and happiness. They remove rheumatism and keep the three humours, wind, bile and phlegm in proper proportion. They purify and strengthen the nerves of the legs and thighs. They are suitable for keeping up Brahmacharya.

SECTION THREE

MUKHYA ASANAS

5. SIRSHASANA

Sirshasana is known by other names as Kapalyasana, Vrikshasana (like a tree), Viparitakarani and Topsy-turvy pose. This is the king of all Asanas.

TECHNIQUE

Spread a fourfold blanket. Sit on the two knees. Make a finger-lock by interweaving the fingers. Place it on the ground up to the elbow. Now, keep the top of your head on this finger-lock or between the two hands. Slowly raise the legs till they become vertical. Stand for five seconds in the beginning and gradually increase the period by 15 seconds each week to 20 minutes or half an hour. Then slowly bring the legs down. Strong people can remain in this Asana for half an hour within a period of 2 or 3 months' practice. Do it slowly. Do not be anxious. Be calm. Be cool. There is eternity before you. On this score do not be sluggish in your practice. Do this Asana on an empty stomach. If you have time, do twice daily both morning and evening. Perform this Asana very, very slowly and avoid jerks. While standing on the head, breathe slowly through the nose and never through the mouth.

You can place the hands on the ground one on each side of the head. You will find this easy to practise if you are fat. When you learn balancing, then you can take to finger-lock method. This Asana is nothing for those who can do balance in parallel bars or on the ground. Ask your friend to assist you to keep the legs steady while practising or get the help of a wall when you begin to learn this.

In the beginning, some may have some sensation during practice but soon this vanishes. It brings joy and glee. After the exercise is over take a little rest for five minutes and then take a cup of milk. Those who do this Asana for a long time, say, 20 minutes or half an hour, should take some kind of light refreshment, milk or anything, when this Asana is over. This is very important. This is *sine qua non.* In summer do not practise this Asana for a long time. In winter you can practise as long as you desire.

There are people who are doing this Asana for two or three hours at one stretch. Pandit Raghunath Sastri of Badrinarayan was very fond of this Asana and used to practise it for 2 or 3 hours. There was a Yogi at Varanasi who entered into Samadhi in this Asana. Sri Jaspat Rai, P.V. Acharyaji Maharaj, and others, were doing this Asana regularly for more than one hour daily at one stretch.

BENEFITS

This is very useful in keeping up Brahmacharya. It makes you an Urdhvaretas. The seminal energy is transmuted into spiritual Ojas-Sakti. This is also called sex-sublimation. You will not have wet dreams, spermatorrhoea. In an Urdhvareto-Yogi the seminal energy flows upwards into the brain for being stored up as spiritual force which is used for contemplative purposes (Dhyana). When you do this Asana, imagine that the seminal energy is being converted into Ojas and is passing along the spinal column into the brain for storage. Sirshasana invigorates, energises and vivifies.

Sirshasana is really a blessing and a nectar. Words will fail to adequately describe its beneficial results and effects. In this Asana alone, the brain can draw plenty of Prana and blood. This acts against the force of gravity and draws an abundance of blood from the heart. Memory increases admirably. Lawyers, occultists and thinkers will highly appreciate this Asana. This leads to natural

Pranayama and Samadhi by itself. No other effort is necessary. If you watch the breath, you will notice that it becomes finer and finer. In the beginning of practice, there will be slight difficulty in breathing. As you advance in practice, this vanishes entirely. You will find real pleasure, exhilaration of spirit, in this Asana.

Great benefit is derived by sitting for meditation after Sirshasana. You can hear Anahata sounds quite distinctly. Young, robust persons should perform this Asana. The advantages that are derived from this Asana are incalculable. Those who practise this should not have frequent copulation.

This is a panacea, a cure-all, a sovereign specific for all diseases. It brightens the psychic faculties and awakens Kundalini Sakti, removes all sorts of diseases of the intestines and stomach and augments mental power. This is a powerful blood-purifier and nervine tonic. All diseases of the eye, nose, head, throat, stomach, genito-urinary system, liver, spleen, lungs, renal colic, deafness, gonorrhoea, diabetes, piles, asthma consumption, syphilis, etc., are cured. It augments the digestive fire, Jatharagni. Wrinkles and grayness will disappear. "He who practises this for three hours daily conquers time"—*Yoga Tattva Upanishad.* Even ladies can practise this Asana. Many uterine and ovarine diseases are cured. Sterility disappears. Asana, Pranayama and Japa should go hand in hand. Repeat the Mantra of your Ishta Devata or the Mantras given by your Guru during the practice of this Asana.

Remember always the precious words of Lord Krishna: "Tasmat Yogi Bhava"—"Therefore become thou a Yogi" (Gita, Chapter VI-46).

Sri Prakash Jung, Private Secretary to the late Maharaja of Tehri State, Himalayas, had swelling of feet and disease of heart. The muscles of the heart were not able to contract and dilate properly in its function of pumping. That was the diagnosis of the doctors. He practised Sirshasana regularly for a few days. All swelling disappeared. The heart functioned properly. There was no pain at all. He used to do this Asana for half an hour daily.

Pandit Surya Narayan, Advocate, Lakhimpure Kheri, was doing this Asana. His memory has been considerably improved. The pain in the back and shoulders (chronic rheumatism) vanished completely.

VARIETIES

I. Vrikshasana:

II. Viparitakarani Mudra:

III. Kapalyasana:

The Sirshasana, described above, is also called by these three names.

IV. Ardha Vrikshasana:

As you stand in Sirshasana, just fold the legs at the knee-joint and keep them along with thighs.

V. Mukta Hasta Vrikshasana:

Instead of making the finger-lock, keep the hands on the ground, by the side of the head.

VI. Hasta Vrikshasana:

You will have to stand on the two hands alone in this Asana. First throw your legs on the walls, standing on your hands only. Slowly try to take the legs away from the walls. In a few days you will learn balancing.

VII. Ekapada Vrikshasana:

After performing the Sirshasana, slowly bend one leg at the knee and keep the heel over the other thigh.

VIII. Urdhva Padmasana

6. SARVANGASANA

(All-Members' Pose)

This is a mysterious Asana which gives wonderful benefits. This is termed "all-members' pose," because all the parts of the body are engaged when this Asana is performed.

TECHNIQUE

Spread a thick blanket on the floor and practise this Asana over blanket. Lie on the back quite flat. Slowly raise the legs. Lift the trunk, hips and legs quite vertically. Support the back with two hands, one on each side. Rest the elbows on the ground. Press the chin against the chest and form a chin-lock firmly, Jalandhara Bandha. Allow the back, shoulder portion and neck to touch the ground closely. Do not allow the body to shake or move to and fro. Keep the legs straight. When the Asana is over, bring the legs down very, very slowly with elegance and not with any jerks. Do the Asana very gracefully. In this Asana the whole weight of the body is thrown on the shoulders. You really stand on the shoulders with the help and support of the elbows. Concentrate on the thyroid gland which lies on the front lower part of the neck. Retain the breath as long as you can do with comfort and slowly exhale through the nose.

You can do this Asana daily twice, morning and evening. This should immediately be followed by Matsyasana (fish posture). This will relieve pains in the back part of the neck and intensify the usefulness of Sarvangasana. Practise this Asana for two minutes in the beginning and gradually increase it to half an hour.

BENEFITS

In this Asana, the thyroid gland is nourished properly which plays a prominent part in the metabolism, growth, nutrition and structure. Healthy thyroid means healthy function of the circulatory, respiratory, alimentary, genito-urinary and nervous systems of the body. This thyroid operates in conjunction with other ductless glands, pituitary, pineal in the brain, suprarenal above the kidneys, liver, spleen, testes. If this thyroid is diseased all the other glands suffer. A vicious circle is formed. Sarvangasana keeps a healthy thyroid. Healthy thyroid means healthy functioning of all the organs of the body.

I have taught this Asana to hundreds of persons. I have started a Sirsha-Sarvanga Propaganda. I generally recommend these two Asanas, combined with Paschimottanasana invariably to those who approach me. These three Asanas alone can keep you in perfect health. You need not take any long walk or physical exercise. All have unanimously reported to me of the wonderful, mysterious, beneficial results of this Asana. As soon as you come down from the Asana, it braces you up and gives a new vigorous, healthy tone. It is an ideal "pick-me-up".

It supplies a large quantity of blood to the spinal roots of nerves. It is this Asana which centralises the blood in the spinal column and nourishes beautifully. But for this Asana there is no scope for these nerve-roots to draw sufficient blood-supply. It keeps the spine quite elastic. Elasticity of the spine means everlasting youth. It prevents the bone from early ossification (hardening). So you will preserve and retain your youth for a long time. This Asana destroys the ravages of old age. It helps a lot in maintaining Brahmacharya. Like Sirshasana, it makes you an Urdhvareto-Yogi. It checks wet-dreams effectively. It acts as a powerful blood tonic and purifier. It tones the nerves. It is a cheap, readily available blood, nervine and digestive tonic. It is at your disposal at all times. It will save your doctor's bills. When you have not much time to practise a course of Asanas, do this without fail daily along with Sirshasana and Paschimottanasana. It is useful in gonorrhoea and other diseases of bladder and ovaries. It removes sterility and diseases of womb. Ladies also can practise this Asana with safety. Sarvangasana awakens Kundalini and augments the Jatharagni (digestive fire). It removes dyspepsia, constipation and other gastro-intestinal disorders of a chronic nature. It energises, invigorates and vivifies. A course of Sirsha-Sarvangasana powerfully rejuvenates.

7. HALASANA
(Plough Pose)

When this pose is practised, it gives the exact appearance of a plough. Hala means a plough in Sanskrit.

TECHNIQUE

Spread a blanket on the ground. Lie flat on your back. Keep the hands at the sides on the ground with the palm facing the ground. Join both your legs. Lift them up very slowly. Do not bend the legs. Do not raise the hands. Do not bend the trunk. Make an obtuse angle. Then slowly lower the legs. Fold them over the body until the toes touch the ground. Keep the knees quite straight and close together. The legs and thighs must be in one straight line. Press the chin against the chest. Breathe slowly through the nose only and not through the mouth.

There is another variety of doing this Asana. After the above posture is done, slowly bring the hands and catch hold of the toes. This is also a better method. There should be no jerk in any way. When the Asana is finished, very, very slowly raise the legs and bring them to the original posture of lying flat on the ground.

BENEFITS

This Asana tones the spinal nerves, the muscles of the back, the vertebral bones and the sympathetic nervous system that runs along the vertebral column on both sides. This Asana fulfils and amplifies Sarvangasana. A large quantity of blood is poured into the spinal roots of nerves, spinal cord, sympathetic ganglia, sympathetic nerves and muscles of the back. Hence, they are all well nourished. The vertebral column is rendered very, very soft and elastic. This Asana prevents the early ossification of the vertebral bones. Ossification is quick degeneration of bones.

Old age manifests quickly on account of early ossification. The bones become hard and brittle in the degenerative process. He who practises Halasana is very nimble, agile, full of energy. The muscles of the back are alternatively contracted, relaxed and then pulled and stretched. Hence they draw a good supply of blood by these various movements and are well nourished. Various sorts of myalgia (muscular rheumatism), lumbago, sprain and neuralgia are cured by this Asana.

The vertebral column becomes soft and elastic. It is twisted and rolled as it were like a piece of canvas sheet. A man who practises Halasana can never become lazy. The vertebral column is a very important structure. It supports the whole body. It contains the spinal cord, spinal nerve and sympathetic system. In Hatha Yoga the spine is termed as Meru Danda. Therefore you must keep it healthy, strong and elastic by the practice of Halasana. The muscles of the abdomen, the rectal muscles and the muscels of the thigh are also toned and nourished. Obesity or corpulence and habitual or chronic constipation, gulma, congestion and enlargement of the liver and spleen are cured by this Asana.

VARIATIONS

Utthana Padasana:

Lie down. Keep the legs straight and the hands by your sides, the palms facing the ground. Raise the two legs together about two feet from the ground without bending the legs and the knees. Slowly bring them down. Repeat this six times. Constipation, pain in the hips and thighs will be removed. This is a preliminary exercise of Sarvangasana.

8. MATSYASANA
(Fish Pose)

As this Asana will help one to float on water easily with Plavini Pranayama, it is called fish pose or Matsyasana.

TECHNIQUE

Spread a blanket and sit on Padmasana by keeping the right foot over the left thigh and the left foot over the right thigh. Then lie flat on the back. Rest the head on the crossed forearms. This is one variety.

Stretch the head back so that the top of your head rests on the ground firmly on one side and the buttocks only on the other, thus making a bridge or an arch of the trunk. Place the hands on the thighs or catch the toes with the hands. You will have to give a good twisting to the neck. This variety is more efficacious than the former one. The benefits that you derive from this variety are a hundred times more than what you get in the previous variety.

Fatty persons with thick calves, who find it difficult to have Padmasana (foot-lock) may simply sit in the ordinary way and then practise this Asana. Practise the Padmasana first. Make it firm, easy and steady. Then take to Matsyasana. Do this Asana for 10 seconds to start with and increase it to 10 minutes.

When you have finished the Asana, slowly release the head with the help of the hands and get up. Then unlock the foot-lock.

You must practise this Asana soon after Sarvangasana. It will relieve stiffness of the neck and any crampy condition of the cervical region caused by long practice of Sarvangasana. This gives natural massage as it were or shampooing to the congested parts of the neck and shoulders. Further, it affords the maximum benefits of Sarvangasana. It supplements Sarvangasana. As the larynx or wind-box and trachea (wind-pipe) are thrown open widely, this Asana helps deep breathing. The apices of the lungs which are located just behind and above the clavicular bone (or collar bone in common parlance), receive proper air and sufficient supply of pure oxygen. The cervical and upper dorsal nerves are nourished with a good quantity of blood and toned properly. The endocrine glands, viz., pituitary and pineal, that are located in the brain are stimulated and toned also. These glands play a vital part in the physiological functioning of the various systems of the body.

BENEFITS

Matsyasana is the destroyer of many diseases. It removes constipation. It brings down the accumulated faecal matter to the rectum. It is useful in asthma, consumption, chronic bronchitis, etc., on account of the deep breathing.

9. PASCHIMOTTANASANA

Sit on the ground and stretch the legs stiff like a stick. Catch the toes with the thumb, index and middle fingers. While catching, you will have to bend the trunk forwards. Fatty persons will find it rather difficult to bend. Exhale and slowly bend without jerks till your forehead touches your knees. You can keep the face between the knees also. When you bend down draw the belly back. This facilitates the bending forwards. Bend slowly by gradual degrees. Take your own time. There is no hurry. When you bend down, bend the head between the hands. Retain it on a level with them. Young persons with elastic spine can touch the knees with the forehead even in their very first attempt. In the case of grown-up persons with rigid spinal column, it will take a fortnight or a month for complete success in the posture. Retain the breath till you take the forehead back to its original position, till you sit straight again. Then breathe.

Retain the pose for 5 seconds. Then gradually increase the period to 10 minutes.

Those who find it difficult to do the full Paschimottanasana, can do half pose with one leg and one hand and then with the other leg and other hand. They will find this more easy. After some days when the spine has become more elastic, they can have recourse to the full pose. You will have to use common sense while practising Asanas. Before you practise this, read the instructions on Janusirshasana.

BENEFITS

This is an excellent Asana. It makes the breath flow through the Brahma Nadi, Sushumna, and rouses the gastric fire. It reduces fat in the abdomen. This Asana is a specific for corpulence or obesity and for the enlargement of spleen and liver. Books on Hatha Yoga speak highly of this Asana. The Sarvangasana is for the stimulation of endocrine glands and Paschimottanasana for the stimulation of abdominal viscera, such as kidneys, liver, pancreas, etc. It increases the peristalsis of the bowels. Peristalsis is the vermicular movement of the bowels or intestines by which food and faecal matter are pushed from one portion of the bowels to another. This Asana relieves constipation, removes sluggishness of liver, dyspepsia, belching and gastritis. Lumbago or stiff back and all sorts of myalgia and other diseases of the back muscles are cured. This Asana cures piles and diabetes also. The hip muscles of the abdomen, the solar plexus of nerves, the epigastric plexus of nerves, bladder prostrate, lumbar nerves, sympathetic cord, are all toned up and kept in a healthy, sound condition. Thanks to Paschimottanasana, Sirshasana and Sarvangasana and to the Rishis who first introduced these wonderful Asanas to the students of Hatha Yoga.

10. MAYURASANA

(Peacock Pose)

Mayur means Peacock in Sanskrit. When this Asana is exhibited, it resembles a peacock which has spread out the bundle of feathers at its back. This is a little more difficult than Sarvangasana and Matsyasana. This demands good physical strength. Gymnasts can do this very easily. This corresponds more or less to plank exercise on the parallel bars.

TECHNIQUE

Kneel on the ground. Squat on the toes. Raise the heels up. Join the two forearms together. Place the palms of the two hands on the ground. The two little fingers must be in close opposition or juxtaposition. The thumbs should touch the ground. They should project towards the feet.

Now you have got steady and firm forearms for supporting the whole body in the ensuing elevation of the trunk and legs. Now bring down the abdomen slowly against the conjoined elbows. Support your body upon your elbows that are pressed now against the navel or umbilicus. This is the first stage. Stretch your legs and raise the feet straight on a level with the head, parallel to the ground. This is the second stage.

Neophytes (beginners) find it difficult to keep up the balance as soon as they raise the feet off the ground. Place a cushion in front. Sometimes you will have a fall forwards and you may hurt your nose slightly. Try to slip on the sides when you cannot keep up the balance. If you find it difficult to stretch the two legs backwards at one stroke, slowly stretch one leg first and then the other. If you adopt the device of leaning the body forwards and head downwards, the feet will by themselves leave the ground and you can stretch them quite easily. When the Asana is in full manifestation, the head, trunk, buttocks, thighs, legs and feet will be in one straight line and parallel to the ground. This posture is very beautiful to look at.

Beginners can practise this Asana by holding the sides of a cot. They will find it easy to practise in this way. If you use your common-sense, you can easily keep up the balance without much difficulty. Fatty people must be cautious to avoid falls or slips. Do not jerk the feet when you stretch them.

Practise this Asana from 5 to 20 seconds. Those who have good physical strength can do for 2 or 3 minutes.

Retain the breath when you raise the body. It will give you immense strength. When you finish the Asana, exhale slowly.

BENEFITS

Mayurasana has got a charm of its own. It braces you up quickly. It gives you full exercise within a few seconds. It serves like a hypodermic injection of Adrenalin or Digitalin.

This is a wonderful Asana for improving the digestion. It destroys the effects of unwholesome food. It increases the digestive power. It digests even the terrible Halahala poison and destroys its terrible effects. It cures dyspepsia and diseases of stomach like Gulma (chronic gastritis), and reduces splenic and liver-enlargement by increasing the intra-abdominal pressure. The lungs and whole abdominal Viscera (organs) are properly toned and stimulated by the increase of intra-abdominal pressure. Sluggishness of liver or hepatic torpidity disappears. It tones the bowels, removes constipation (ordinary, chronic and habitual) and awakens Kundalini.

It gives wonderful appetite, removes all diseases caused by an excess of wind, bile or phlegm, cures diabetes, hemorrhoids and strengthens the muscles of the arms. This one Asana can give you maximum physical exercise in the minimum time.

VARIETIES

I. Lolasana:

Form Padmasana, sit in the first stage of Mayurasana. Now the weight of your body will be on your knees and hands. Then slowly raise your lower part of the body forming the Padmasana. This is a sort of swinging pose with Padmasana. This is termed Lolasana. This is a variety of Mayurasana. The benefits of Mayurasana are derived from this Asana also.

II. Hamsasana:

This is quite an easy Asana. The preliminary portion of Mayurasana is known as Hamsasana. Here the toes are kept on the ground before the legs are raised for Mayurasana.

11. ARDHAMATSYENDRASANA

Ardha means half. This is half a pose. This Asana takes its name from the Rishi or Yogi Matsyendra, who first taught this Asana to the students of Hatha Yoga. This Matsyendra is said to have been the disciple of Lord Siva. Once Siva departed for a lonely island. There He taught Parvati the mysteries of Yoga. A fish that happened to be near the shore heard the teachings of Lord Siva. Siva came to know this. His heart being filled with mercy He sprinkled water on this Yogi-fish. Immediately, on account of Siva's grace, the fish became a Siddha Yogi with a divine body. This Yogi fish was called by the name Matsyendra.

Paschimottanasana and Halasana bend the spine forwards. Dhanurasana, Bhujangasana and Salabhasana are counterposes to bend the spine backwards. This is not sufficient. It must be twisted and bent from side to side also (literal movements). Then only perfect elasticity of the spinal column can be ensured. Matsyendrasana serves this purpose well, in giving a lateral twist to the spinal column. Some Hatha Yogins start with this Asana when they give practical lessons to the Yogic students.

TECHNIQUE

Place the left heel near the anus and below the scrotum. It can touch the perennial space. Do not allow the heel to move from this place. Perennium is the space between the anus and the external organ of generation. Bend the right knee and place the right ankle at the root of the left thigh and rest the right foot well on the ground, close to the left hip joint. Place the left Axilla arm-pit over the top of the vertically bent right knee. Push the knee now a little to the back so that it touches the back part of the Axilla. Catch hold of the left knee with the left palm. Then applying pressure at the left shoulder-joint, slowly twist the spine and turn to the extreme right. Turn the face also to the right as much as you can do. Bring it in a line with the right shoulder. Swing round the right arm behind the back. Catch hold of the left thigh with the right hand. Retain the pose from 5 to 15 seconds. Keep the vertebral column erect. Do not bend. Similarly, you can twist the spine to the left side. This will complete the spinal twist.

BENEFITS

This Asana increases appetite by increasing the digestive fire. It destroys terrible diseases. It rouses Kundalini and makes the Chandranadi (moon) flow steadily. The moon is said to be located above the root of the palate. It drops the cool ambrosial nectar, which is wasted by mixing with gastric fire. But this Asana prevents it.

It keeps the spine elastic and gives a good massage to the abdominal organs. Lumbago and all sorts of muscular rheumatism of the back muscles are cured. The spinal nerve-roots and sympathetic system are toned. They draw a good supply of blood. This Asana is an auxiliary to Paschimottanasana.

12. SALABHASANA

(Locust Pose)

When this pose is demonstrated, it resembles a locust. Hence the name Salabha, a locust.

TECHNIQUE

Lie on the ground, face downwards. Keep the hands by the sides. the palms should be turned up.

You can place the hands underneath the belly also. This is another way. Inhale (Puraka) slightly. Retain the breath (Kumbhaka) till you finish the Asana and then exhale slowly. Stiffen the whole body and raise the legs in the air one cubit high. Raise the head as in Bhujangasana. Keep the thighs, legs and toes as shown above. Turn up the soles of the feet. Lift up the legs, thighs and lower portion of the abdomen. Keep up this pose from 5 to 30 seconds. Bring the legs down slowly. Now exhale very, very slowly.

You can repeat the process 6 to 7 times. You can keep the hands near your chest on the ground, with the palms facing the ground.

BENEFITS

This Asana gives a posterior curvature to the spine. It bends the spine backwards. In bending the spine it serves as a counter-pose to Paschimottanasana, Halasana and Sarvangasana which bend the spine forwards (anteriorly). Like Mayurasana, it increases the intra-abdominal pressure. It supplements the Bhujangasana. Bhujangasana develops the upper half of the body, while Śalabhasana develops the lower half of the body and the lower extremities also. It tones up the muscles of the abdomen, thighs and legs. It brings down the accumulated faecal matter of the stomach to ascending colon, from ascending colon to transverse colon of large intestines, from transverse colon to descending colon and from there to the rectum. Read any book on elementary physiology. It will help you a lot.

This Asana gives a good exercise for the abdomen. It relieves constipation. It tones the abdominal viscera (organs) viz., liver, pancreas, kidneys, etc. It removes several diseases of the stomach and bowels. It cures sluggishness of liver and hunchback. the lumbo-sacral bones are toned up. Lumbago is removed. All forms of myalgia of the lumbar region (hips) are removed. The digestive fire is increased. Dyspepsia is removed. You will have very good appetite.

13. BHUJANGASANA

(Cobra Pose)

Bhujanga means a Cobra in Sanskrit. When this pose is exhibited, the raised head and trunk resemble the raised hood of a cobra. Hence this is called Bhujangasana.

TECHNIQUE

Spread a blanket on the ground. Lie flat downwards keeping the back above. Relax all the muscles. Be at ease. Place the palms on the ground just below the shoulders and elbows. Let the body from the navel downwards to the toes touch the ground. Raise the head and upper portion of the body slowly just as the cobra raises its hood. Bend the spine backwards. Now the muscles of the back and lumbar regions are well stretched. The intra-abdominal pressure is also increased. Then slowly bring down the head to its original position. When you lie down at first with the face downwards on the ground, the chin is pressed against the chest. The chin-lock is formed. Repeat the process of raising the head and bringing it down half a dozen times, steadily. Breathe slowly through the nose. Retain the breath till you raise the head and bend the spine properly. Then you can slowly exhale. Then retain the breath while bringing the head down. As soon as the head touches the ground, breathe again slowly.

BENEFITS

Bhujangasana bends the spine backwards (posterior curvature) while Sarvangasana and Halasana bend it forwards (anterior curvature). This relieves hunchback, back pain, lumbago, myalgia of the back. It increases the intra-abdominal pressure and brings down the loaded faecal matter from the transverse colon to rectum. Hence it relieves constipation. It increases bodily heat and destroys a host of ailments. It awakens the Kundalini that is sleeping dormant in the Muladhara Chakra. It gives good appetite.

Bhujangasana is particularly useful for ladies in toning their ovaries and uterus. It is a powerful tonic. It will relieve amenorrhoea (absence of menstruation,) dysmenorrhoea (painful or difficult menstruation), leucorrhoea (whites), and various other utero-ovarine diseases. It keeps up efficient blood-circulation in those parts and is more powerful than Aleteris Cordial. Deliveries will be normal and easy.

14. DHANURASANA

(Bow Posture)

When this Asana is performed, it represents the appearance of a bow (Dhanus). The stretched arms and forelegs form the string of the bow. It bends the spine backwards. It supplements Bhujangasana. We can say it is a combination of Bhujangasana and Salabhasana with the addition of catching the ankles with the hands. Bhujangasana, Salabhasana and Dhanurasana form a valuable combination. They always go together. They form one set of Asanas. This combination acts as a counter-pose to Halasana and Paschimottanasana, which bend the spine forwards.

TECHNIQUE

Lie on your chest with the face downwards. Relax all the muscles. Keep the arms at the sides. Gently fold the legs at the back. Raise your hands backwards. Catch hold of the ankles with the hands. Raise the chest and head. Expand the chest. Keep the arms and forelegs quite straight and stiff. Now a good convex arch is formed. If you stretch the legs, you can raise your chest up. You should dexterously manipulate. Retain the breath in a mild manner and exhale slowly. Do this 5 or 6 times. You can retain the pose as long as you can comfortably keep it. Keep the knees close.

The whole body rests on the abdomen. This Asana gives a good massage to the abdominal region. You must do this Asana when the stomach is empty. You can give a good movement to the bow-shaped body from side to side, laterally and forwards and backwards. They will ensure a thorough massage to the abdomen. Swing, rock and rejoice. Mentally repeat Om, Om, Om.

BENEFITS

This is useful in chronic constipation, dyspepsia and sluggishness of liver. It removes hunchback, rheumatism of legs, knee-joints and hands. It reduces the fat, energises digestion, increases peristalsis, invigorates the appetite and relieves congestion of blood in the abdominal viscera and tones them also.

Dhanurasana is a blessing for people who suffer from gastro-intestinal diseases. Like Halasana it keeps the spine elastic. It prevents premature ossification of bones. He who does Halasana, Mayurasana and Dhanurasana can never become lazy. He is full of energy, vigour and vitality.

VARIETIES

I. Akarshana Dhanurasana:

This Asana can be termed as Dhanurasana. Sit on the ground. Spread the legs. Catch the right toe with the left hand. Slowly bend the left leg and bring the toes to your chin level and the knee near the left armpit. Now the thigh will touch closely your abdominal portion. Catch hold of the left toe with the right hand and keep the elbow at the back as far as possible. This is more beneficial than the previous variety.

15. GOMUKHASANA

(Cow-Face Posture)

When this Asana is demonstrated, it will look like the face of a cow. Hence this significant name. Gomukha means 'Cow-face.'

TECHNIQUE

Place the heel of the left leg under the left part of the anus. Bring the right leg in such a way that the right knee will be above the left knee and the right sole along the side of the left thigh in close contact. By gradual practice, you will have to bring the right heel to touch the left buttock. Sit quite erect. Now you will have to make a finger-lock of the two index-fingers at the back dexterously, of course with a little difficulty in the beginning. Take the left hand to the back, raise the left index-finger upwards. Bring the right index-finger downwards and catch hold of the left index-finger firmly. Make a finger-lock now. If it slips, try again, and keep the lock for two minutes. Breathe slowly. The Asana will now look like the face of a cow. When you make the finger-lock, do not turn the body, do not bend the heel and chest. Keep the trunk quite straight. Change the hands and legs alternately. Fat people will find it difficult to do this Asana, to adjust the heels and thighs and to make the finger-lock. But continual practice will make them all right.

BENEFITS

This Asana removes rheumatism in the legs, sciatica, piles or haemorrhoids, neuralgia of the legs and thighs, indigestion, dyspepsia, muscular pain in the back, and sprain in the forearms. This helps in maintaining Brahmacharya and good health. Mula Bandha comes by itself and can be kept up with ease. Hence, this Asana is suitable for the practice of Pranayama. Ordinarily you can sit at all times in this Asana for long meditation also. Lean persons with thin thighs and legs will like this Asana very much. Yogi

Swami Svarupananda of Jwalapur, Haridwar, was a votary of this Asana. He used to sit always in this Asana alone. This was his favourite Asana. If you find a little congestion (accumulation) of blood in the thighs and legs, massage or shampoo the legs and thighs with your hands as soon as you release the Asana.

There is also another variety of Gomukhasana. When you do this variety, raise the elbow of the left hand upwards and the fingers at the back. Take the right hand to the back, raise the index-finger up as far as you can and form a hook of the index-fingers.

VARIATIONS

I. Vama Janvasana:

You will have to keep the legs as in Gomukhasana by keeping the right thigh and knee over the left. The hands can be kept near your chest or on the lap of knees.

II. Dakshina Janvasana:

In this Asana the left thigh and knee are kept over the right. This is convenient for some persons.

16. VAJRASANA

(The Adamantine Pose)

Those who sit in this Asana have a steady, firm pose. They cannot be easily shaken. The knees are rendered very hard. The Meru Danda becomes firm and strong. This Asana resembles more or less the Namaz pose in which Muslims sit for prayer.

TECHNIQUE

Keep the soles of the feet on both sides of the anus i.e., place the thighs on the legs one over the other and the soles on the buttocks. The calves must touch the thighs. The part from the toe to the knee should touch the ground. The whole burden of the body is put on the knees and ankles. In the beginning of practice, you may feel a slight pain in the knee and ankle joints but it passes off very quickly. Massage the paining parts and the two joints with the hands. You can use a little Iodex or Amritanjan for rubbing. After the feet and the knees, put both the hands straight on the knees. Keep the knees quite close. Sit like this, keeping the trunk, neck and head in one straight line. This is the most common Asana. You can sit in this Asana for a very long time comfortably. Yogins generally sit in this Asana.

BENEFITS

If you sit in this Asana for about half an hour immediately after food, the food will be digested well. Dyspeptics will derive much benefit. The nerves and muscles of the legs and thighs are strengthened. Myalgia in the knees, legs, toes and thighs disappears. Sciatica vanishes. Flatulence is removed. The stomach works vigorously. The practice of Vajrasana exercises a stimulating, beneficial influence on Kanda, the most vital part, and which is situated 12 inches above the anus and from which 72,000 Nadis spring.

VARIATIONS

Some people will keep the heels quite separate. The anus and the buttocks are kept between the two heels and the legs by the side of the two thighs.

I. Kurmasana (Tortoise Pose):

Press the buttocks firmly with the soles. Keep the head, neck and trunk erect. Keep the hands on your hips or on the knees or on the sides of the chest.

II. Ardha Kurmasana:

Sit in the same Vajrasana and stretch your hands to your face level, palms facing together and slowly bend and lie down on the ground on the support of your hands.

III. Utthana Kurmasana:

In this, you will have to sit in the same way as you sit for Garbhasana by keeping the hands between the calves and thighs. In Garbhasana, the feet are kept on the thighs as in Padmasana; but in Uttana Kurmasana the ankles are kept quite close one over the other and the hands pressing the head down. By all these Asanas, sprains and pains in the back will disappear.

IV. Mandukasana (Frog Pose):

Take the feet towards the back. Let the toes touch each other. Place the knees at the sides. Keep the hands on knees. This is called Mandukasana.

V. Ardha Savasana:

See the instructions elsewhere under Supta Vajrasana.

VI. Padadirasana:

Some people call the Vajrasana as Padadirasana. In this pose you can keep the hands on the knees or to your chest level, palms facing each other.

VII. Parvatasana:

Sit in Vajrasana posture. Raise your body and the hands above your head very slowly. This is called Parvatasana. A better variety of Parvatasana is described elsewhere.

VIII. Ananda Mandirasana:

Sit in Vajrasana and catch hold of the heels with the two hands.

IX. Angushthasana:

This is an important Asana for keeping up Brahmacharya. By sitting in Vajrasana slowly raise your knees. There is a similar Asana. See the description of Padangushthasana elsewhere.

X. Supta Vajrasana:

This is sleeping pose and Vajrasana combined or same as Ardha Savasana. First you must be perfect in doing Vajrasana. Then you can take to this Asana. More strain and force come on the knees in this Asana than in

Vajrasana. Lie down on the back as in Ardha Savasana. Make a finger-lock. Allow the head to rest on the palms. Instead of making a finger-lock, you can place the hands as instructed in Matsyasana (first variety). In the beginning, the entire portion of the back may not touch the ground. The lower portion will remain raised up. Within a few days' practice, you will be able to do this Asana quite satisfactorily.

In this Asana you will get all the advantages of Vajrasana. Hunchback is removed as the spine is bent backwards. The spine gets elastic also. He who does this Asana will find it easy to do Chakrasana.

Ordinary Siddhasana also is known as Vajrasana.

17. GARUDASANA

(Eagle Pose)

When this Asana is demonstrated it resembles the appearance of Garuda, the eagle. Hence it is called Garudasana.

TECHNIQUE

First stand up quite straight. Place the right leg straight on the ground. Raise up your left leg and take it round the right leg. The left thigh should cross the right thigh. Just as the creeper encircles or winds round a tree, so also the left leg should wind around the right leg. Keep hands (arms) also likewise, one arm winding round the other. The palms of the hands should touch each other. Make the fingers like the beak of an eagle. Keep the hands just in front of the face. Change the legs and hands alternately.

When you stand as instructed above, steadily bend and try to touch the ground with the toe of the leg that encircles. Then alone, you can get the maximum benefits of this Asana. You can take the help of somebody when you bend down. Both the legs have to be bent. You can do Basti (cleansing the bowels with water) in this Asana.

BENEFITS

The whole weight of the body comes on one leg in this Asana, whereas in Kukkutasana the whole weight of the body comes on the two hands. The nerves and bones of the legs and hands are strengthened. The hands and legs are lengthened. A man may grow tall by the practice of this Asana. The nerves of the kidneys also are strengthened. Sciatica, rheumatism of the legs and hands are cured. The bones of the vertebral column get developed and strengthened. Hydrocele and swelling of the testicles are cured. The muscles of the calves get developed. The nerves of the legs and hands are strengthened.

18. URDHVA PADMASANA

TECHNIQUE

Perform Sirshasana as mentioned before. Slowly bend the right leg and keep it on the left thigh and then the left leg on the right thigh. You must do this very carefully and slowly. If you can stand in Sirshasana for more than 10 or 15 minutes, then alone you can attempt this. Otherwise, you will have a fall. A gymnast who can balance himself on the parallel bars or on the ground can do this Asana quite easily. The practice of this Asana needs some strength. Breathe slowly through the nose and never by the mouth. Remain in the posture from 5 to 10 minutes in the beginning and gradually increase the time.

To start with practice this Asana by the side of a wall over a fourfold blanket. There are some other varieties in this Asana. They are not of much use.

Some persons will find it easy to do Padmasana first and then they will raise the legs slowly. Experienced persons can bring down the Padmasana to the ground and again they can raise the legs above as before. Those who practise this Asana should take some light tiffin, a cup of milk or fruit juice after finishing this Asana. Practitioners of Sirshasana and Urdhva Padmasana should keep up Brahmacharya. Then only will they realise the maximum benefits.

BENEFITS

When any sort of prayer or Japa is done during the course of Asanas, it becomes a Tapas also. You will get Siddhis. In days of yore, Tapasvins used to stand on the head for a period of twelve years and repeat the Mantras of the Ishta Devata or Guru. You will find this in Maha Bharata in many instances. Japa or meditation in Urdhva Padmasana or Sirshasana touches the heart of the Lord deeply. He showers His blessings quickly. Many difficulties will be obviated. All the advantages of Sirshasana are derived from this Asana. He who practises this will have perfect control over the body.

Pandit Sri Suryanarayan, Advocate, Lakhimpur, practised this Asana. His memory had considerably increased. It cured spermatorrhoea or wet-dreams in Ganga Prasad, a student of M.Sc. class, and Narendra, a student of the Calcutta Medical College. Judge Kedarnath could turn out double the work in Courts and read books for many hours. You can also sincerely practise this Asana regularly and get the full benefits and live long in perfect health.

19. PADANGUSHTHASANA

Fatty people will find it a little difficult to practise this Asana. They are tossed about either from siue to side or forwards and backwards. A little steady practice will make matters all right. In former days the Naishthika Brahmacharins of Gurukulas used to practise this Asana daily. Rishis of yore prescribed this Asana along with Sirshasana and Sarvangasana for Brahmacharins for the preservation of Virya, or the vital energy.

TECHNIQUE

Put the left heel right in the centre of the anus or perennium, the space between anus and external organ of generation. Put the whole weight of the body on the toes, particularly the left big toe. Place the right foot over the thigh near the knee. Sit carefully now, keeping up balance. If you find it difficult to practise this Asana independently, you can take the help of a bench by placing your hands on the bench or sitting by the side of a wall. Place the hands on the sides of the hips. Retain the breath as long as you can do it comfortably. Breathe slowly. Gaze steadily on any black or white spot in front of you. Repeat your Guru Mantra or Rama Rama while practising the Asana.

BENEFITS

The perennial space is four inches in breadth. Underneath this space lies the Virya Nadi or the spermatic duct that carries the semen or vital energy from the estes. By pressing the Nadi with the heel, the flow of semen outside is checked. A steady practice of this Asana removes wet-dreams or spermatorrhoea and makes one an Urdhvareto-Yogi or a Yogi in whom the semen flows upwards to the brain and gets stored up there as Ojas-Sakti or spiritual power. A combination of Asanas such as Sirshasana, Sarvangasana, Siddhasana, Bhujangasana and Padangushthasana is very conducive to keep up Brahmacharya. Each has its own specific action. Siddhasana and Bhujangasana act on the testes and its cells and prevent the formation of semen. Sirshasana and Sarvangasana help the flow of semen towards the brain. Padangushthasana acts on the spermatic duct effectively.

20. TRIKONASANA

(Three Angle Pose)

TECHNIQUE

Stand erect. Keep your legs two feet apart. Now stretch your arms wide on the sides in a line with the shoulders. The arms must now be quite parallel to the ground. You might have done this portion of the exercise in your drill class in the school. Now bend slowly to the right. Keep the left knee stiff and erect. This is important. Touch the right toe with the fingers of the right hand. Bend the neck slightly to the right. It may touch the right shoulder. Now stretch the left arm above. Retain the posture for 2 or 3 minutes. Breathe slowly. Again you can practise on the left side. Let the fingers of the left hand touch the left toe. Stretch the right arm in the air as before. Do 3 or 6 times on each side.

BENEFITS

This Asana gives very good lateral movements to the spine. It is an auxiliary Asana to Ardha Matsyendrasana. It amplifies and fulfils the Matsyendrasana. Mr. Muller also gives a description of this Asana in his system of physical culture exercises. If you have a healthy spine, you can sit in your meditation in one Asana for many hours without fatigue. For a Yogi the spine or Meru Danda is a great thing as it is connected with the spinal cord and the sympathetic system. It is the spine that contains the important Sushumna Nadi which plays a vital part in the Kundalini movement. This Asana tones the spinal nerves and the abdominal organs, increases peristalsis of the bowels and invigorates appetite. Constipation is relieved. The body becomes light. Those who suffer from shortening of the leg due to fracture of hip or thigh bone (Femur) or bones of the leg (Tibia or Fibula) will be benefited by this Asana. This Asana lengthens the legs. Krishna Kumar Bhargava, Advocate, Sitapur, practised this Asana for three months. His legs became lengthened and he was able to walk one or two miles later.

21. BADDHA PADMASANA

(Locked-up Lotus Pose)

This is a variety of Padmasana (Lotus Pose).

TECHNIQUE

Sit in Padmasana with legs crossed. The heels should touch the lower part of the belly or abdomen. Then take your right hand behind the back. Catch hold of the right leg with the forefinger and middle finger of the right hand. Then take your left hand behind the back and catch hold of the toe of the left leg with the forefinger and middle finger of the left hand. Now press the chin against the chest. Look at the tip of the nose, Nasikagra Drishti. Breath slowly.

Some people find it difficult to catch hold of the two toes at a time. They can practise Ardha Baddha Padmasana (half-pose) to start with for a month. Afterwards they can take to the Purna Baddha Padmasana (full-pose). Practise this Ardha Baddha Padmasana on the right side. Then do alternately on the left side also. In doing the full pose, use little skill. Catch one toe first and when you attempt to catch the other one, slightly bend the body forwards. This will make matters easy in catching the other toe. During the half-pose, catch hold of one toe with one finger. Change the side afterwards. The half-pose is a preparatory stage for the full-pose.

This is not an Asana for meditation. This is chiefly intended for improving the health, vigour and vitality of the body to a considerable degree. The benefits of the Padmasana are derived in this Asana to an enormous extent. This must be practised regularly at least for six months. Then only maximum advantages can be realised. You cannot expect the full benefits of this Asana by merely sitting for a couple of minutes. You must practise this at least for half an hour. If you can do it for an hour or an hour and a half, you will doubtless derive immense benefit. There are persons who do this Asana for full three hours. How tenacious and patient these people are! They keep wonderful health and vigour and a high standard of vitality. Many diseases are cured by this Asana. Chronic diseases of the stomach, liver, spleen and intestines that are pronounced incurable by Allopaths and Ayurvedic Kavirajas are cured by a steady practice of this Asana. There is no doubt of this. Diseases of the stomach such as chronic gastritis, dyspepsia, flatulence, colic, dysentery, ascites, constipation, acidity, belching, chronic lumbago, are removed. As it keeps the Meru Danda erect, hunch-back is removed. The nerves of the waist, hip, feet and legs are purified. Enlargement of the spleen and liver is cured. Torpidity of the liver disappears. This Asana exercises a potent influence over the Surya Chakra (solar plexus of nerves) behind the Nabhi (navel) and stimulates it. You draw a great deal of energy.

Draw the belly backwards and upwards. Repeat Om or Rama mentally. Imagine that the seminal energy flows towards the brain for being stored up as Ojas-Sakti. Do this special practice for 10 minutes daily. You will have no wet-dreams. This process is a great help for keeping up Brahmacharya.

22. PADAHASTASANA

(The Feet and Hands Posture)

This can be styled as "Standing Paschimottanasana," as the technique is the same. The only difference is that you will have to do this while standing. Some people call this "Hastapadangasana."

TECHNIQUE

Stand erect. Let the hands hang down closely by the sides. Keep the heels close and toes apart. Raise the hands above the head. Slowly bend the body downwards. Keep the knees stiff and erect. Do not bend the legs at the knees. Slowly bring the hands down without bending at the elbows and catch hold of the toes with your thumb, index and middle fingers only. When you bend, slowly exhale and draw the belly backwards. Keep the forehead between the knees. The face is buried between the hollow of the knees or the head can be pushed further between the two thighs. There are varieties in this Asana by interchanging the feet and hands. There is no space here for a detailed description. Further, they are not of much use or advantage. Retain the pose from 2 to 10 seconds. Fatty people will find it difficult to practise this Asana in the beginning. With patience and perseverance they will be able to do it perfectly in a short time. When you draw the back, you will have to contract the abdominal muscles and rectum.

If you find it difficult to catch hold of the toes owing to the stiffness of the muscles of the hips and excess of fat in the abdomen, bend the knees slightly. After catching hold of the toes, straighten and stiffen the legs. That is Yukti or common-sense. You can drink a small quantity of water before you do this Asana.

BENEFITS

There are manifold benefits of this Asana. You will feel much invigorated after the exercise is over. The body is rendered light as much Tamas is dispelled. Adiposity disappears. Any shortening of the legs owing to fracture of the leg or thigh-bones is rectified. You will get slight lengthening of the leg by practice of this Asana for about three months and rubbing the thighs and legs with mustard oil to which a little salt is added. Salt increases penetration of the oil. This Asana helps free passage of Apana Vayu downwards. The Sushumna Nadi is purified and strengthened. The benefits of Paschimottanasana are derived from this Asana also.

VARIATIONS

I. Padahastasana (Second Variety):

Stand erect. Slowly raise your left leg and catch hold of the toe with your fingers. Keep the right on your hip. Do not bend the legs. Some people call this variety as Padahastasana.

II. Tadasana (Tree Pose):

This is a familiar exercise among the school-students in the drill-class. Now raise one hand above the head very quickly. Do not bend the head. Then bring it to former position. Again do the same with the other hand. Repeat like this as many times as you can. Instead of taking directly above the head at one stretch, you can stop for a while when the hand comes to your shoulder level, parallel to the ground. You can take the two hands together also. When this Asana is over, shampoo the muscles of the hands, shoulders, etc. This Asana is also called Vrikshasana. Sirshasana is also called Vrikshasana. Stand erect on one leg keeping the other leg at the root of the other thigh. This is also a variety of Vrikshasana.

III. Utthita Vivekasana:

This is very useful for doing Pranayama and Japa in standing position. Stand erect. You can keep the hands in a folded way near your chest.

IV. Purna Padasana:

If you keep your hands at sides and stand erect, it is called Purna Padasana.

23. MATSYENDRASANA

(Full Pose—Spine Twist)

Those who have practised Ardha Matsyendrasana for some time are ready for taking up this full pose. The full pose is a little more difficult than the half pose. The late Sri Madhavadasji Maharaj of Malsar (Gujarat), a famous Hatha Yogi, used to teach his students this pose straightaway. This Asana derives its name from the Rishi Matsyendra.

TECHNIQUE

Sit erect with legs stretched. Place the left foot on the joint of the right thigh forcibly with both your hands and fix the heel of the left foot at the navel. Let the right leg touch the ground by the side of your left knee. Place the left hand outside the right knee and press the knee to the left side. Get hold of the right toe with the fingers (thumb, index and middle fingers) of the left hand. The right foot should remain firm. Turn the right hand towards the back and catch hold of the left heel. The face and body are turned back towards the right side. Twist the spine. Gaze at the tip of the nose. Breathe slowly. Retain the pose for 20 seconds. You can keep it for 2 or 3 minutes also by gradual practice. Repeat the process several times. The technique appears to be difficult. If you give careful attention and think with concentration, then it is very clear and easy. Or see once when your friend does this Asana.

This should be practised both by the right side and left side by turns. Then only maximum benefits of the Asana will be derived. First do the half pose for 2 or 3 weeks and then attempt this. Then the muscles and joints will be more elastic and flexible. If you find it difficult to keep up your balance, instead of turning your hand towards the back, you can keep the palm on the ground. This will give you good support, and would make matters easy. Slowly you can take the hand away and turn it towards the back.

BENEFITS

The advantages that are derived from the half pose will be derived in this full pose to a great extent. The synovial fluid of the joints increases and the joints become very active. All the adhesions in the joints that are caused by rheumatism are removed. It bestows beautiful health. It augments the Prana Sakti (vigour and vitality) and consequently removes innumerable diseases. The pressure of the heel on the navel forces blood towards the back which nourishes well all the nerves of the back, particularly the Prana Nadis of the back. It awakens the Kundalini and brings peace of mind. Hail! Hail! the Yogi Matsyendra who first introduced this Asana amongst the Hatha Yogic students. *Om Namah Parama Rishibhyah*—Prostrations to the Rishis!

24. CHAKRASANA

(Circle Pose)

Many acrobats demonstrate this Asana in the streets. Young boys can do this Asana very easily because their spine is very elastic. When the bones become rigid and ossified in advanced years, bending of the spine becomes difficult. It resembles a circle. Hence the significant name Chakrasana. In fact, it resembles more a bow than a circle.

TECHNIQUE

Stand up. Raise the hands above in the air. Slowly bend towards the back making a curve of the body. When the hands come to your hip-level at the backside, slowly bend your legs at the knee. This will help you to bend further and to touch the ground with your hands. Do not be in a hurry. Do it slowly by adjusting balance. Otherwise, you will have a fall. Keep a thick blanket on the ground and over this, practise this Asana. In the beginning, you can do this by the side of a wall or you can ask your friend to catch hold of your hips firmly and then bend.

There is another way of doing the Asana. This is suitable for old people. There is no danger of falling at all. Lie down on the back. Keep the soles and palms on the ground. The palms must be kept by the side of your head and the elbow above. Now bring your heels near to your palms on the ground and raise your body above, thus making a curve of your spine. By continuous practice one can render the spine very elastic. Elasticity of spine means everlasting youth. A man with a rigid spine can form a semicircle at the outside. In the course of two weeks all the rigid parts will become elastic. You can catch hold of the heels with the hands when you do this Asana.

BENEFITS

He who practises this Asana will have perfect control of the body. He will be agile and nimble. He can turn out more work in a short space of time. All the parts of the body are benefited by this Asana. If you find it difficult to keep the Asana for a long time, lie down flat on the ground, again lift it up. When you raise yourself upon this Asana the body will be light. You will get exhilaration of spirit at once. You will be ready for active work. If there is any pain in the neck and shoulders after the practice of Sarvangasana, do this Asana immediately for a few minutes. It will relieve the pain as it bends the neck backwards and thus it is a counter-pose to Sarvangasana. All the other benefits of Dhanurasana, Salabhasana and Bhujangasana are derived from this Asana.

25. SAVASANA

(Corpse Pose)

This is an Asana for relaxation of all muscles, nerves, etc. This Asana should be performed at the very end. It is a closing pose. Mritasana is another name for this pose.

TECHNIQUE

Spread a soft blanket. Lie flat on your back. Keep the hands on the ground by the sides. Stretch the legs quite straight. Keep the heels close. Let the toes remain separated. Close the eyes. Breathe slowly. Relax all muscles, nerves, organs, etc. Start the relaxation process from the toes. Then proceed to the calf-muscles, muscles of the back, chest, arm, forearm and hands, neck, face, etc. See that the abdominal organs, heart, chest, brain are also relaxed. Relax the plexus of nerves also. Now repeat "Om, Om, Om." Think of Atman. Think of Rama. Meditate gently with Suddha Bhava, feeling of purity. Do not sleep. Continue the meditation for 15 minutes. You will enjoy perfect peace, ease, comfort and relaxation. Every one of you should enjoy it. Words are imperfect. They cannot adequately describe the feelings.

BENEFITS

Savasana combines pose and meditation. It gives rest not only for the body but also for the mind and soul. It gives relief, comfort and ease. Relaxation is a very important factor in muscular exercises. In Halasana, Sarvagasana, Paschimottanasana, Dhanurasana and Ardha-Matsyendrasana, you know pretty well that all the muscles of the back, Lettissimus dorsi, Psoasmagnus, Quadratus lumborum, Rectus, abdominis, Pectoralis major of the chest, Biceps, Triceps, the deltoid of the arm, Sartorius of the thighs, are all stretched and contracted to an enormous degree. During intense muscular activity, the metabolism is increased. Metabolism is the Anabolic and Catabolic changes that take place in the body (wear and tear in the system). Anabolic changes are constructive and Catabolic changes are the destructive ones. During metabolism all the muscular tissues are supplied with fresh oxygenated blood or plasma through capillary oozing and carbon dioxide is taken back through the veins to the right auricle of the heart. This is termed tissue-respiration. Just as interchange of oxygen and carbo dioxide takes place in the lungs, so also interchange of carbon dioxide and oxygen takes place in the tissues also. Mark the wonderful creation and working of the internal mechanism of the body! How marvellous is the machinery! Can a scientist make a single atom, a single cell, a single organ of the body? Bow with folded hands before the Creator of this wonderful mechanism of the body. Repeat Om Ram. Enter into silence. Meditate. The whole mystery of creation will be revealed unto you through His Grace.

The muscles that are put under severe strain demand relaxation and rest. It is Savasana that promptly and efficiently ensures complete relaxation and perfect ease.

SECTION FOUR

MISCELLANEOUS ASANAS

26. JANUSIRSHASANA

(Head-Knee Pose)

TECHNIQUE

Sit down. Press the perineal space with your left heel, stretching your right leg at full length. Keep it quite straight. Catch hold of the foot with both hands. Exhale. Draw the belly inwards. Slowly bend down the head and touch your right knee with the forehead. Keep the position for 5 to 10 seconds. Gradually increase the period. You can do the Asana even for half an hour by steady practice.

Then slowly raise the head to its former, normal position. Take rest for a few minutes. Again practise this Asana. Do like this 5 or 6 times. Change the sides alternately. When, you practise, retain the nerves of the anus upwards. Feel that seminal energy is flowing upwards to the brain as Ojas Sakti. Use your Bhavana Sakti of the mind. Those who practise this Asana will find it easy to practise Paschimottanasana.

Instead of taking the heel to the perineum, you can put it on the thigh. This is a little more difficult than the previous one. Practise this Asana after evacuating the bowels.

BENEFITS

This Asana increases the digestive fire and helps digestion. It stimulates the solar plexus, Surya Chakra, and helps you in keeping up Brahmacharya. All urinary troubles are cured. It is very useful for the intestinal colic. Kundalini is awakened. Laziness and weakness will vanish.

You will be very energetic. The legs are strengthened. All the other benefits mentioned in Paschimottanasana can be derived from this Asana also.

27. TOLANGULASANA

(Weighing Scale Pose)

This Asana when demonstrated will resemble the form of a weighing scale. Hence this is named as Tolangulasana.

TECHNIQUE

Lie down in Padmasana as in Matsyasana. Place the palms of the hands underneath the buttocks. If you find it difficult to keep the palms below the buttocks, slowly rest on your two elbows by gradual reclining. Raise the head and the upper part of your body above the ground. Now the whole body will be resting on the buttocks and forearms. Press the chin against the chest. This is Jalandhara Bandha as you can comfortably keep and then exhale slowly. You can do this 5 to 30 minutes.

BENEFITS

This Asana removes flatulence. Meru-Danda is expanded and developed. Owing to the tension of the abdomen, the faecal matter is pushed down to the rectum from the colon. As the chest considerably expands, the pigeon-chest is slowly removed and you will have a broad, fine chest. You will obtain the benefits of Padmasana. The muscles and the nerves of the arms and forearms get increased supply of blood. Therefore, they will become strong.

28. GARBHASANA

(Child-in-the-Womb Pose)

When this Asana is demonstrated, it resembles the position of the child when it is in the womb. Hence this is called Garbhasana.

TECHNIQUE

As described in Kukkutasana introduce both hands in the space between the thighs and calves. Bring out the elbows of the two hands. Catch hold of the right ear with the right hand and the left ear with left hand. You should perform the last stage of the Asana with great care. Because when you try to catch hold of the ears with the hands, you may fall down backwards. You will have no hands to support the body and you will be helpless. But by practice you can slowly balance the body on the buttocks. The body will remain steady after a few days' practice. If you find it difficult to perform the Asana, you can do it without the Padmasana. Catch hold of the ears or neck by introducing the arm behind the thighs. In this modified pose the legs will be stretching downwards. Remain in the Asana for 2 or 3 minutes. Repeat it five times.

BENEFITS

The digestive power is augmented. Appetite increases. The bowels become quite free. You will get clear motions. Many intestinal diseases are removed. Hands and legs will become strong.

29. SASANGASANA

Bend the legs and stand on your toes and knees. Keep the palms by the side of the soles. Make a perfect curve of the back and bend down your head towards the ground. Do not bend the hands. Keep them straight. This is similar to Dhanurasana. You can call it Dhanurasana or Chakrasana in a standing posture. The benefits of Dhanurasana are derived in this pose.

30. SIMHASANA

(Lion Pose)

Place the two heels under the scrotum or between the anus and the scrotum, the left heel on the right side and the right heel on the left side. Keep the hands between the thighs. Open your mouth. This is the destroyer of diseases. This is practised by Yogins. The Bandhas can be nicely practised in this Asana.

31. KUKKUTASANA
(Cock Pose)

In Sanskrit, Kukkuta means a cock. When the Asana is demonstrated it resembles a cock.

TECHNIQUE

First do Padmasana. Introduce your two arms one by one as far as the elbow joint into the space between the calves. Place the palms on the ground, fingers pointing forwards. Raise the body from the ground as shown in the picture. The lock of the feet should come as far as the elbow joint. If you raise the Padmasana a bit, it will be easy to introduce your hands. Fatty persons will find it difficult to insert the hands between the thigh and calf muscles. Remain in this Asana as long as you can.

BENEFITS

All the benefits of the Padmasana can be derived from this Asana to a maximum degree. Alasya (laziness) vanishes. The Nadis get purified. Biceps of the hands, deltoid of the shoulders, pectoralis major and minor, etc., are developed well. The chest becomes broad. Then hands get lengthened.

32. GORAKSHASANA

Turn the face upward and place it in a hidden manner between the thigh and calf muscles. Cover the heels by the hands. Do Jalandhara Bandha. Have Nasikagra Drishti. This Asana gives success to the Yogis.

33. KANDAPIDANASANA

TECHNIQUE

This Asana is a bit difficult for people with big thigh

and calf muscles. Lean persons can do this very beautifully. Sit on the ground, heels and the toes together. That is, the soles must be facing each other. Slowly twist the feet and place the heels at the perineum and the toes towards the back at the anus. Now the body will rest only on the two knees and the sides of the feet. Keep the hands on the knees. Sit erect. There is another way of doing this Asana. Sit on the ground with the soles of the feet in close opposition. They also must be facing each other. Take hold of the toes of one foot with both the hands and slowly attempt to take the foot to the belly. In a similar manner bring slowly the other foot also to the belly. When you are able to do this Asana with each foot separately, then try to do it with both the feet at one stroke. Practise this Asana gradually with great care. If you do it quickly with force, you will get pain in the legs, knees, toes etc. When the Asana is complete, the soles will be diverging and the dorsal (back) sides of the feet will be facing each other.

BENEFITS

All sorts of knee troubles, rheumatism of the legs, sciatica, gout of the toes will be cured. The nerves of the calves and legs will be toned. Fatty people will find it difficult to practise this Asana.

34. SANKATASANA

Stand on right foot. Raise the left leg and surround it over the right. Keep the hands on the knees. This is Sankatasana. Garudasana posture also is called by this name.

35. YOGASANA

Keep the right foot on the left thigh and left foot on the right thigh, soles turning upwards. Place the hands on the ground by your sides, palms facing upwards. Gaze at the tip of the nose, and meditate for a long time.

36. UTKATASANA

Stand up. Keep the feet close together. Keep the hands on the hips, one on each side. Then slowly lower the body. You will experience a little difficulty when you lower the body down. In the beginning you can catch hold of the sides of the two doors to your hip level and then with their support, lower the body. You can take the help of the two arms of a chair also. He who practises Pranayama can practise this Asana very easily. This Asana does not require much strength. One should know balancing of the body. A thin man with a wiry body can do this very beautifully. When you lower the body, you may lose the balance and the body may be tossed either laterally or anterio-posteriorly. But a few days' practice will enable you to keep up the posture steady. When you perform the Asana perfectly, your legs from toes to knees and the part of the body from the buttocks to the head will be in a perpendicular line to the ground and your thighs will be in a parallel line with the ground. In the beginning when you practise this Asana, you can sit in a chair. Slowly raise the body two or three inches above the chair and try to keep up the balance. After a few days, ask your friend to remove the chair silently and try to keep up the balance. Sit on the toes. The whole burden of the body is placed on the toes only. The buttocks will touch the heels. Lumbago is cured. Wrists and toes are strengthened. This is very useful for elephantiasis. You can lower the body still further as shown in the second variety. This pose is used for Basti Kriya.

37. JESHTHIKASANA

This is an exercise for relaxation like Savasana. This must be done in the end of all the Asanas. This is similar to Savasana. In this Asana the hands are kept on the ground by the sides of your head, while in Savasana the hands are kept at the sides.

38. ADHVASANA

Lie down quite flat, keeping the belly and chest on the ground. The hands will be at sides, palms facing the ground. Stretch the body well. This is a reverse pose of Savasana with the same benefits. For some time keep the right cheek on the ground and for some time the left cheek.

39. URDHVAPADASANA

This is another name for "Uttana Padasana". For instructions, see elsewhere.

40. USHTRASANA

(Camel Pose)

Lie on the ground face downwards. Turn the legs and keep them over the thighs. Catch the toes or ankles with your hands. You can raise the head a bit above. This is similar to Dhanurasana, but the thighs are kept on the ground in this Asana. The benefits of Dhanurasana and Salabhasana can be had in this pose.

41. MAKARASANA

(Dolphin Pose)

Lie on the ground face downwards as in Adhvasana. Catch hold of the head with the hands.

42. BHADRASANA

(Gentle Pose)

Sit at ease. Keep the body erect. Press the two heels firmly against the sides of the perineum or at the anus. Fix the gaze at the tip of the nose. This destroys all diseases and the effects of poison.

43. VRISCHIKASANA

(Scorpion Pose)

Those who can practise the Sirsha or Hasta-Vrikshasana well for a long time, can attempt this Asana. Keep the hand and elbows on the ground. In the beginning, practise this Asana by the side of a wall. Now throw the legs on the wall and try to keep up the balance after taking the feet two inches away from the wall. Do like this for a few days. When you are able to keep up the balance, slowly bend the legs at the knee and hips towards the back and place your soles or toes on your head. All the benefits of Sirsha, Chakra and Dhanur Asanas can be had in this Asana to a maximum degree.

44. YOGA NIDRASANA

Lie down as in Savasana. Fat people cannot do this Asana. They need not try this. Take hold of the legs and fix the feet below the neck or head. Then slowly raise the buttocks and keep the palm on the ground below the buttocks or hips.

45. ARDHAPADASANA

Sit on the ground. Place the right heel near the right buttock and the left ankle on the right knee. Keep the hands on the ground a few inches away from the buttocks. Similarly do this for the other leg also.

46. KOKILASANA

Sit on Sama or Siddha Asana. Keep the hands firm at the arm-pits. Now the elbows will be in a line. Slowly bend and place the elbows on the ground in front of you. The weight of the whole body will remain on the two buttocks and elbows. Do this Asana over a blanket. Otherwise the elbows will be injured.

47. KARNAPIDASANA

Perform Halasana keeping the hands on the floor at the back. Now slowly bend the legs at the knees and bring the knees to touch your shoulders. In this Asana the leg from the knees to the toes will be parallel to the ground.

48. VATAYANASANA

Stand erect. Take hold of the right foot and place the heel firmly at the root of the thigh or at the root of the organ and stand on one leg. Slowly bend the left leg and let the right knee touch the ground. This is Vatayanasana.

49. PARYANKASANA

Ordinary Supta Vajrasana described elsewhere is known by this name.

50. MRITASANA

This is another name for Savasana. See the instructions elsewhere.

SPECIAL INSTRUCTIONS

1. Asanas should be practised in a well-ventilated, clean room where there is free movement of fresh air. The floor must be even. Asanas can be practised on the sandy bed of rivers, open airy places and by the sea-side also. If you practise them in a room, see that the room is not congested so as to allow free movement of hands, legs and of the body.

2. Asanas should be done on empty stomach in the morning or at least three hours after food. Morning time is best for doing Asanas.

3. It is always better to start Japa and Meditation in the early morning at 4 a.m., as soon as you get up from bed. At this time the mind is quite calm and refreshed. You can catch the meditative mood now quite easily. Meditation is more important. In the early morning, as soon as you get up from bed, the mind is like a clean slate, free from worldly thoughts. The mind will enter into the meditative mood without effort or struggle.

4. The vast majority of persons waste their precious time in the early morning in answering the calls of nature for half an hour and washing their teeth for another half an hour. The sun rises before they sit for meditation. This is bad. Aspirants should try to defecate within five minutes and cleanse their teeth within five minutes. If the bowels are constipated have vigorous practice of Salabha, Bhujanga and Dhanur Asanas for five minutes as soon as you get up from bed. If you are habituated to answer the calls of nature late in the day, you can do so after finishing Asana and Pranayama, Japa and meditation.

5. Get up at 4 a.m. Answer the calls of nature. Wash your face. Then practise your Asanas, Pranayama and Meditation. This order is beneficial. If you are very particular to meditate from 4 to 6 a.m., you can do Sirshasana

for 10 to 15 minutes and then sit for meditation. When meditation is over, you can take to other Asanas. If you are not in the habit of answering the calls of nature in the early morning, you can practise Asanas without answering the calls. After finishing the Asanas and Meditation you can go to the latrine. Then motion also will be free.

6. Those who suffer from chronic constipation, can practise GANESA KRIYA, removal of excreta by introducing the middle finger lubricated with soap or oil into the rectum. Occasional douching will be beneficial to empty the loaded stomach.

7. Spread a blanket on the floor and practise the Asanas over the blanket. Use a pillow or four-folded blanket for practising Sirshasana and its varieties.

8. Wear a Langoti or Kowpina or suspendary bandage when you practise Asanas. You can have a banian on the body.

9. Do not wear spectacles when you do Asanas. They may be broken and may injure your eyes.

10. Those who practise Sirshasana, etc., for a long time should take light tiffin or a cup of milk after finishing the Asana.

11. If you can devote half an hour or more to Sirshasana alone, you can cut short the time for other Asanas.

12. Be regular in the practice. Those who practise by fits and starts will not derive any benefit.

Mitaharam vina yastu yogarambham tu karayet,
Maharogo bhavettasya kinchid yogo na sidhyati.

(Ghe. S. Chap. V-10)

Without observing moderation of diet, if one takes to the Yogic practices, he cannot obtain any benefit but gets various diseases.

13. Before starting the practice of Asanas, take a dose

of worm powder santonin, gr. 1 or 2 at bed time and castor oil 2 oz., early in the next morning. Float the oil in peppermint water, tea or pepper water and then take. Take oil alone if you like. Thorough cleansing of the bowels is necessary when you take to the Yogic practices.

14. Start with minimum time of doing Asanas and then gradually increase the period. You can do the Asanas as long as you can comfortably keep up the posture.

15. Asana is the third Anga in Ashtanga Yoga. When you are established in Asanas, then only you will derive the benefits of Pranayama.

16. Maximum benefits can be achieved if Japa also is done during the practice of Asanas and Pranayama.

17. If the foundation of a building is not properly laid, the superstructure will fall down in no time. Even so, if a Yogic student has not gained mastery over the Asanas, he cannot successfully proceed in his higher course of Yogic practices.

18. Regularity in the practice is very necessary if one wants to realise the maximum benefits of Asanas. Generally, people practise for two months in the beginning with great interest and enthusiasm and leave off the practice. This is a sad mistake. They want a Yogic teacher always by their side. They have got the effeminate leaning mentality. They are lazy, torpid and slothful.

19. Nowadays, outdoor games have become very costly. Nets, rackets, balls, inflators have to be purchased again and again. No expense is needed for the practice of Asanas.

20. Physical exercises draw the Prana out. Asanas send the Prana in, and distribute it quite evenly throughout the body and different systems. Asanas are not only physical but also spiritual, as they awaken the Serpent Power that is sleeping in the Muladhara Chakra. This is the third

Anga (limb) of Ashtanga Raja Yoga of Patanjali Maharshi. A particular Asana removes a particular disease.

21. Asanas are not mere physical exercises alone. They are something more than that. They have a spiritual basis. They help a long way in controlling the senses, mind and body. Body-nerves and muscles are purified (Sarira Suddhi and Nadi Suddhi). Kundalini is awakened which gives Bliss, Power and Yogic Samadhi to the aspirant. If you do Dand and Bhaitaks (native physical exercises) 500 times a day or pumping marches on the parallel bars 50 times a day for 5 years, they will not in any way help in the awakening of this mysterious power, Kundalini. Do you see the difference now?

22. Ladies also should practise Asanas. They will have healthy and strong children. If mothers are healthy and strong, children also will be healthy and strong. Regeneration of the young ladies means the regeneration of the whole world. If ladies practise a course of Asanas systematically with interest and attention, they will have wonderful health and vitality. There is no doubt of this. I hope they will give patient hearing to my earnest and sincere prayer and start practising these Asanas from the very day they read these Yogic lessons. Glory to these new Yogic lady students who tread the path of Yoga. Children born of Yoginis will also be Yogins.

23. Japa and Pranayama should go hand in hand with Yoga Asanas. Then it becomes a real Yoga.

24. In the beginning you cannot perform some of the Asanas perfectly. Regular practice will bring perfection. Patience and perseverance, earnestness and sincerity are needed.

25. Sirsha, Sarvanga, Paschimottana, Dhanur and Mayura Asana are a good combination. Sirsha, Sarvanga and Paschimottana are the trinity Asanas. You can reduce the number of Asanas if you cannot spare time. These

three Asanas will give you all the advantages and benefits of all other Asanas.

26. Four Asanas are prescribed for Japa and Meditation, viz., Padma, Siddha, Svastika and Sukha Asanas. Padmasana is the best for the vast majority. Those who attempt to keep up Brahmacharya should practise Siddhasana.

27. Never change the Asanas. Adhere to one set tenaciously. If you do one set of Asanas today and some other tomorrow and so on, you cannot derive much benefit.

28. The more steady you are in the Asana, the more you will be able to concentrate and make your mind one-pointed. You cannot get on well in your meditation without having a steady posture.

29. Common-sense should be used throughout your practice. If one kind of food is not agreeable to your system, change it after due consideration or consultation with your Guru. If a particular Asana is not suitable, select something else. This is Yukti. Where there is Yukti, there is Siddhi, Bhukti and Mukti (perfection, enjoyment and liberation).

30. If you cannot perform a particular Asana quite satisfactorily, do not lose heart. Where there is a will, there is a way. Rome was not built in a day. Remember the story of Bruce and the Spider. Try, try, try again. Continuous practice will make you all right.

31. No Samadhi or superconscious state is possible without awakening the Kundalini. Kundalini can be awakened by various ways, viz., Asanas, Mudras, Bandhas, Pranayama, Devotion, Grace of Guru, Japa, strong analytic will and Vichara Sakti. Those who attempt to awaken the Kundalini should have perfect purity in thought, word and deed. They should have mental and physical Brahmacharya. Then only can they enjoy the benefits of Samadhi. When Kundalini is awakened, the old Samskaras are

loosened and the Hridayagranthi (heart-knot of ignorance) will be cut asunder. You will be freed from the wheel of Samsara (birth and death) and will attain Immortal Satchidananda state eventually.

32. Mild Kumbhaka (retention of breath) during the practice of Asanas augments the efficacy of Asanas and gives increased power and vitality to the practitioner.

33. Those who practise Japa can repeat the Mantra during the practice of Asanas. When you recite the Mantra for six months, a habit will be formed and the force of Samskara will keep up the uninterrupted practice even during the performance of Asana. There will be no difficulty. Business people who have very little time at their disposal, can have Japa during their practice of Asanas. It is something like getting four fruits by throwing one stone only. You will get many Siddhis.

34. Those who practise Sirshasana and its varieties should take some light tiffin, a cup of milk or fruit-juice after the Asana is over. Tiffin is absolutely necessary when they practise for a long time. They will have to keep up their Brahmacharya strictly.

35. Everyone should select a course of a few Asanas to suit his temperament, capacity, convenience, leisure and requirement.

36. It is advisable that Yogic students should practise all Asanas after attending to the calls of nature. If you are in a habit of defecating in the afternoon or evening only, you should change this habit anyhow. You must be able to get one clear motion in the early morning as soon as you get up from bed. Go to the closet regularly and sit there for a short time at 4 a.m. You may fail to get a motion for a few days at that time. After some days you will have a regular motion. A habit will be formed. Yogis can break any old habit in no time and establish a healthy, new habit. Drink some cold or lukewarm water at night and in

the early morning also as soon as you get up. Regulate and adjust the diet also. You can meditate in the morning as soon as you get up and then you can do Asanas.

37. If you are careful about your diet, Asanas and meditation, you will have fine, lustrous eyes, fair complexion and peace of mind in a short time. Hatha Yoga ensures beauty, health, strength and long life to the Yogic students.

38. Avoid unnecessary worry. Do not be troubled. Be not anxious. Do not be idle. Do not waste time. Do not worry yourself if there is delay in your progress. Wait coolly. You are bound to succeed if you are sincere.

39. Never miss a day in your Sadhana, spiritual practices.

40. Do not shake the body unnecessarily. By shaking the body very often, the mind also is disturbed. Do not scratch the body every now and then. The Asana should be as firm as a rock.

41. Breathe slowly. Do not change seat very often. Sit in the same place at the same time every day. Have the right kind of mental attitude as taught by your Guru.

42. The Samsaric Vasana that has arisen through the practice of many hundreds of lives never perishes except through the practice of Yoga for a long time.

43. Never care for Siddhis. Shun them ruthlessly. They will bring your downfall.

44. Yama and Niyama are the foundations of Yoga. If you are fully established in these, Samadhi will automatically follow.

45. You must not give leniency to the mind. If you allow the mind to take one luxury today, it will demand two tomorrow. Luxuries will increase daily. It will become an overfondled child. "Spare the rod and spoil the child." This applies to the mind also. It is worse than a child. You

will have to punish it by fasting for every serious mistake it does. Mahatma Gandhiji did like this. So he had become pure. He had made his will pure, strong and irresistible. Keep the organs at their proper places. Do not allow them to move even an inch. By practice, get a concentrated mind.

46. If you have a careful eye over your defects, if you are sincere and if you struggle, they are sure to vanish sooner or later. Destroy the impurities one by one, little by little, completely.

47. Drink water through the mouth, send it to the stomach and small intestines and make it pass through the anus at once as in enema. This is termed Sanga Pachara Kriya in Hatha Yoga. Even the smoke of a cigarette can be passed through the anus. Brahmachari Sambhunathji of Kishkindha did this. Yogi Trilinga Swami of Varanasi was very clever in Sanga Pachara Kriya. The help of Nauli and Basti Kriya is needed in Sanga Pachara. There is no difficulty at all in the path of Yoga for sincere practitioners.

48. Drink one seer of water through the mouth or nose. Keep it for 20 seconds. Then bring out slowly. This is Kunjara Kriya or Kunjara Yoga. This is a cleansing process of the stomach. This serves a free laxation for the stomach. All the decomposing matters that undergo fermentation in the stomach will come out. You will have no disease of the stomach. Do it occasionally. Do not make it a habit. This is a Hatha Yoga Kriya.

49. People do not want to remove Mala (impurity) by selfless service, and Vikshepa by Upasana (worship). They at once jump to awaken the Kundalini and raise the Brahmakara Vritti. They will only break down their legs. Serve and worship. Do Purushartha. Jnana or Moksha will come by itself. Kundalini will be awakened by itself.

50. A man can sit for 13 hours at one stretch motionless on one Asana and yet he may be full of desires. This

is a mere physical practice like an acrobatic or circus feat. A man without closing the eyes, without winking, without turning the eye-balls, can practise Trataka for three hours and yet he may be full of desires and egoism. This is also another kind of physical exercise. This has nothing to do with spirituality. People are deceived when they see persons who can do the above practices. Fasting for 40 days is also another kind of training of the physical body.

51. Sow the seed of spirituality when you are young. Do not waste the Virya. Discipline the Indriyas and mind. Do Sadhana. Concentrate. Purify. Meditate. Serve. Love. Be kind to all. Realise. When you become old, you will be free from anxiety and fear of death. It is very difficult to do any rigid Sadhana in old age. Therefore, be on the alert during your teens.

52. Do not think any more of your worldly concerns than is necessary to determine your duty. Do your duty and leave the rest to God.

53. You will see for yourself in a short time the particular benefits you derive from particular kinds of Sadhana.

54. The practice of Asanas before starting Japa and Meditation is very good and conducive. It removes laziness and drowsiness of the body and mind. It steadies the mind. It fills the mind with new vigour and peace.

55. Nauli and Uddiyana alone cannot give you Moksha. It is a means for keeping good health. Do not make it the be-all and end-all. The *summum bonum* of life is Realisation of Atman. Purify your mind, concentrate and meditate.

56. You have got all the materials inside for wisdom, for becoming a Yogi or Jnani. Practise. Develop. Assert. Realise.

57. If a man wishes to prosper in life, he must give

up gambling, drinking, excessive sleep, drowsiness, fear, anger, indolence and procrastination.

58. When you advance in spiritual practice, you must observe strict Mouna (vow of silence) for 24 hours continuously. This must be continued for some months.

59. Observe moderation in eating, drinking, sleeping and in everything. The middle path is always good and safe. Observe the golden medium. Then you can become a Yogi soon.

60. Sadachara (pure conduct), Sadvichara (right enquiry), and Satsanga (good company) are necessary during the practice of Yoga.

61. Abandoning all acid, bitter and saltish food, taking delight in drinking milk and Rasa, practising celibacy, being moderate in eating and ever bent on Yoga, the Yogi becomes a Siddha in a little more than a year.

62. Sattvic food is necessary when you practise Asanas and Pranayama. Take milk, Ghee, sweet curd, fruits, almonds, cream, etc. Give up garlic, onions, meat, fish, smoking, liquors, sour and pungent articles. Overloading must be avoided. Take Mithahara. Be regular and punctual in taking meals. Eating all sorts of things at all times is highly dangerous for a Yogi.

63. You must use only a few selected things for your food such as Dhall, Ghee, wheat-flour, potatoes or milk and fruits.

64. You must have Niyama in your food. Control of the tongue means control of the mind. You must not allow the tongue to run riot.

65. Practice of celibacy is very necessary. Food must be Sattvic. Chillies, tamarind, hot curries, Chutnies should be avoided.

66. Brahmacharya is very, very important. Evil thoughts are the beginning of adultery. The very idea of

lust must not enter the mind. You can do nothing, nothing in the path of Yoga without Yama, Niyama, Viveka and Vairagya. Have faith and confidence, interest and attention. You will doubtless succeed.

67. You can never realise God, if you have not got rid of Kamini-Kanchana (lust for women and desires for money), if you are not established in mental Brahmacharya, Satya and Ahimsa.

68. A religious husband and a worldly wife always move in diametrically opposite poles. They cannot enjoy a happy home. The former goes upwards while the latter drags him down. There will always be a tug-of-war between them. There will be no chance for progress in the path of Yoga.

69. He who is attached to his sons, wife, lands and wealth will not derive even an iota of benefit. He is only wasting his precious life and energy. Those who are engaged in endless Sadhana are godly men.

70. Man thinks that he is imperfect if he has not got a wife. After he gets married he again thinks that he is imperfect so long as he has not got a son and a daughter. However much a man may gain materially there is always some sort of discontentment and dissatisfaction. This is universal experience.

71. Should we not try, therefore, to attain the thing more satisfying and eternally lasting? Or should we be content to lead a life of slavery and bondage obeying the impulses of our physical nature?—This question will ultimately arise in everybody's heart if he is a man of common-sense. Everyone must answer this question. It is the starting point of all religions.

72. If you develop Vairagya, if you subdue your Indriyas and sense-enjoyments and pleasures of this world as dung and poison, as they are mixed with pain, sin, fear, craving, miseries, diseases, old age and death, nothing can

tempt you in this world. You will have eternal Peace and infinite Bliss. You will have no attraction for women and other earthly objects. Lust cannot take hold of you.

73. Lust is the greatest enemy on this earth. It devours a man. A great deal of depression follows after copulation. You have to exert a lot in earning money to please your wife and satisfy her wants and luxuries. You commit various sorts of sin in acquiring money. You have to share her pains, troubles and worries. On account of heavy loss of seminal fluid you will suffer from various diseases, depression, weakness and loss of vitality. You will have an early death. Longevity will be unknown to you. Therefore, become an Akhanda (unbroken) Brahmachari.

74. If one kind of Sadhana does not help you in keeping up your Brahmacharya, you should have recourse to a combined method of various Sadhanas, such as Prayer, Meditation, Pranayama, Satsanga, Sattvic food, solitude, Vichara, Asanas, Bandhas, Mudras, etc. Then only you will be established in Brahmacharya.

75. When you walk on the road, do not look hither and thither like a monkey. Loot at the tip of your toe and walk gently with majestic attitude, or look at the ground and walk. This is a great help in maintaining Brahmacharya.

76. Yoga consists in the complete suppression or restraint of the functions of the thinking principle (mind) and the mental modifications.

77. The term 'Yoga' in secondary sense denotes the parts of Yoga and the different actions that go to make up also, as these are the means to the accomplishment of Yoga and indirectly lead to Mukti (final emancipation). Japa, Prayer, Pranayama, Satsanga, study are all Yoga only. This is Gauna, secondary.

78. Asana and Pranayama remove all sorts of diseases, improve health, energise digestion, invigorate the nerves,

straighten the Sushumna Nadi, remove Rajas and awaken the Kundalini. Practice of Asana and Pranayama bestows good health and a steady mind. As no Sadhana is possible without good health, no meditation is possible without a steady mind. Hatha Yoga is of immense use for Dhyana Yogins, Karma Yogins, Bhaktas and Vedantins as well.

79. The Yogi becomes the Master of all forces in nature and can utilise them at will. He has perfect control over the five elements.

YOGIC RECIPE

FOR	ASANAS
1. Meditation and Study	Padmasana, Siddhasana, Svastikasana or Sukhasana
2. Sex-sublimation, Syphilis, Spermatorrhoea, Pyorrhoea, Gonorrhoea, Sterility, Awakening Kundalini, Bad memory, Diabetes, Consumption, Asthma, Renal Colic, Rheumatism, Ear, Eye, Nose troubles, etc.	Siddhasana, Sirshasana, Sarvangasana, Matsyasana or Ardha Matsyendrasana
3. Amenorrhoea, Dysmenorrhoea, Leucorrhoea, Uterine and Ovarine diseases	Sarvangasana, Salabhasana, Paschimottanasana and Bhujangasana (during pregnancy these Asanas should not be done)
4. Chronic Bronchitis	Mastyasana and Salabhasana
5. Disgestion	Sarvangasana, Vajrasana. Paschimottanasana and Baddha Padmasana

6. Liver and Spleen enlargements	Sarvangasana, Halasana, Mayurasana and Baddha Padmasana
7. Chronic Constipation	Halasana, Mayurasana, Dhanurasana, Matsyasana and Padahastasana
8. Hydrocele, Elephantiasis, Shortage of legs and hands	Garudasana, Trikonasana and Utkatasana
9. Piles	Siddhasana, Paschimottanasana, Sirshasana, Gomukhasana and Maha Mudra
10. Dysentery	Baddha Padmasana and Kukkutasana
11. Myalgia and Rheumatism	Vrischikasana, Sirshasana, Paschimottanasana, Sarvangasana, etc.

FOR	ASANA
12. Leprosy	Sirshasana and Maha Mudra
13. Relaxation	Savasana
14. Destroyer of all diseases and bestower of Long Life (Sarvaroga Nivarana and Dirgha-Ayuh-Pradayaka)	Padmasana, Sirshasana, Sarvangasana and Paschimottanasana

N.B.—If you are suffering from some chronic diseases, you will have to combine Mudras, Pranayamas and Japa, also. If a particular item is not suitable to your system, you can consult your Spiritual Guide. You will have to practise them with sincerity and patience for a long time.

SECTION FIVE

IMPORTANT MUDRAS AND BANDHAS

There are several varieties in Mudras and Bandhas, viz., Maha Bandha, Jalandhara Bandha, Uddiyana Bandha, Mula Bandha, and Maha Mudra, Maha Vedha, Nabho, Khechari, Viparita Karani, Yoni, Sambhavi, Asvini, Pasini, Matangi, Kaki, Bhujangini and Yoga Mudras.

Among these I will give you a short description of the few important ones. You can select that which suits you well and practise regularly. Cough, asthma, enlargement of spleen and liver, sex-sublimation, venereal diseases, consumption, chronic constipation, leprosy and all sorts of incurable diseases are also cured. These Mudras and Bandhas will bestow on you all that you want. "*Nasti mudrasamam kinchit samsidhyai kshitimandale*"—There is nothing in this world like the Mudras for giving success.

1. MAHA MUDRA

Press the anus carefully with the left heel. Stretch out the right leg. Catch hold of the toe with the two hands. Inhale and retain the breath (Kumbhaka). Press the chin against the chest firmly, Jalandhara Bandha. Fix the gaze at the Trikuti, Bhrumadhya Drishti. Retain the posture as long as you can. Practise first on the left leg and then on the right leg. This cures consumption, haemorrhoids or piles, enlargement of spleen, indigestion, Gulma (chronic gastritis), leprosy, constipation, fever, etc. Life is increased. It confers Siddhis on the practitioners. When you do this Mudra, the posture will be almost similar to Janusirshasana.

2. YOGA MUDRA

Sit in Padmasana. Place the palms on the heels. Exhale slowly and bend forwards and touch the ground with the forehead. If you retain the pose for a long time, you can breathe in and out as usual, or come to the former position and inhale. Instead of keeping the hands on the heels you can take them at the back. Catch hold of the left wrist with your right hand. This pose removes all kinds of disorders in the abdomen.

3. KHECHARI MUDRA

'Khe' means in sky and 'Char' means to move. The Yogi moves in the sky. Hence this is known as Khechari Mudra.

This Mudra can be performed by a man only if he has undergone the preliminary exercise under the direct guidance of a Guru who is practising Khechari Mudra. The preliminary portion of this Mudra is in making the tongue so long that the tip of the tongue might touch the space between the two eyebrows. The Guru will cut the lower tendon of the tongue with a bright, clean knife, little by little every week. By sprinkling salt and turmeric powder, the cut edges may not join together again. Rub the tongue with fresh butter and draw it out. Take hold of the tongue with the fingers and move it to and fro. Milking the tongue means taking hold of it and drawing it as the milkman does the udder of a cow during milking.

Cutting the lower tendon of the tongue should be done regularly, once a week, for a period varying from six months to two years. By all these means you can lengthen the tongue to reach the forehead. This is the preliminary portion of Khechari Mudra.

Then turn the tongue upwards and backwards by sitting in Siddhasana so as to touch the palate and close the posterior nasal opening with the tongue and fix the gaze at the space between the two eyebrows. The respiration will stop. The tongue is on the mouth of the well of nectar. This is Khechari Mudra.

By practice of this Mudra the Yogi is free from fainting, hunger, thirst and laziness. He is free from diseases, decay, old age and death. This Mudra makes one an Urdhvareto Yogi. As the body of the Yogi is filled with the nectar, he will not die even by virulent poison. This Mudra gives Kaya Siddhi to Yogins. Khechari is the best of all Mudras.

4. VAJROLI MUDRA

This is an important Yogic Kriya in Hatha Yoga. You will have to work hard to get full success in this Kriya. There are very few people who are experts in this act. Yogic students draw water first through a silver tube (catheter, specially made) passed into the urethra (urinary canal) for 12 inches inside, then milk, oil, honey, etc. They draw mercury in the end. Later on they can draw these liquids directly through the urethra without the help of the tube. This Kriya is of immense use in the establishment of Brahmacharya. On the first day you should send the catheter inside the urethra for one inch only, the second day two inches, third day three inches, and so on. You must gradually practise till you are able to send 12 inches of the catheter inside.

Raja Bhartrihari could do this Kriya very dexterously. Even a drop of semen cannot come out of the Yogi who practises this Mudra. Even if it is discharged, he can draw it back through this Mudra. The Yogi who draws his semen up and preserves it conquers death. Good smell emanates from his body. Lord Krishna was a skilled expert in this Mudra. That is the reason why He was called a Nitya Brahmachari though He was amidst several Gopis.

5. VIPARITAKARANI MUDRA

Lie on the ground. Raise the legs up straight. Support

the buttocks with the hands. Rest the elbows on the ground. Remain steady. The sun dwells at the root of the navel and the moon at the root of the palate. The process by which the sun is taken upward and the moon downward is called Viparitakarani Mudra. The positions of the sun and moon are reversed. On the first day do it for a minute. Gradually increase the period to three hours. After six months wrinkles on the face and grey hair will disappear. The Yogis who practise this for three hours daily conquer death. As the gastric fire is increased those who practise this for a long time should take some light refreshment such as milk, etc., as soon as the Kriya is over. Sirshasana posture also is called Viparitakarani Mudra.

6. SAKTI CHALANA MUDRA

Sit in a secluded room in Siddhasana. Draw in the air forcibly and join it with Apana. Do Mula Bandha till the Vayu enters the Sushumna. By retaining the air, the Kundalini being suffocated, awakens and finds its way through Sushumna to the Brahmarandhra. Through the practice of this Mudra one can become a Siddha.

Sit in Siddhasana. Take hold of the foot near the ankle and slowly beat the Kanda with the foot. This is Tadana Kriya. By this method also Kundalini can be awakened.

7. MAHA VEDHA

Sit in Maha Bandha posture explained elsewhere. Draw the breath slowly. Retain the breath. Press the chin against the chest (Jalandhara Bandha). Place the palms on the ground. Rest the body on the palms. Raise the buttocks slowly and strike them gently against the ground. The Asana must be intact and firm when you raise the buttocks. This Kriya destroys decay and death. The Yogi gets control over the mind and conquers death.

8. MAHA BANDHA

Press the anus with the left heel. Place the right foot upon the left thigh. Contract the anus and muscles of the Yoni or perineum. Draw the Apana Vayu upwards. Draw the breath slowly and retain it by Jalandhara Bandha as long as you can. Then exhale slowly. Fix the mind on Sushumna. Practise first on the left side and then on the right side. Generally the Yogi does Maha Mudra, Maha Bandha and Maha Vedha together. This is a good combination. Then only maximum benefits are derived. The Yogi achieves all his desires and obtains Siddhis.

9. MULA BANDHA

Press the Yoni with the left heel. Contract the anus. Forcibly draw upwards the Apana Vayu slowly by practice. Put the right heel on the organ of generation. This is called Mula Bandha, destroyer of decay and death.

The Siddhi or perfection in the practice of Pranayama is attained through the help of Bandhas. The practice of this Mula Bandha helps Brahmacharya, gives Dhatu-Pushti (nerve-vigour), relieves constipation and increases the Jatharagni. He who practises Mula Bandha will keep up everlasting youth. No grey hair will manifest.

The Apana Vayu which does the function of ejection of excreta has a natural tendency to move downwards. Through the practice of Mula Bandha the Apana Vayu is made to move upwards by contracting the anus and by forcibly drawing it upwards. The Prana Vayu is united with the Apana and the united Prana-Apana is made to enter the Sushumna Nadi or Brahma Nadi. Then the Yogi attains perfection in Yoga. This is a secret in Yoga. Then the Yogi is dead to the world. He drinks the nectar of immortality. He enjoys Siva-pada in Sahasrara. He gets all divine Vibhutis and Aisvaryas.

When the Apana is united with Prana, the Anahata sounds or different kinds of Nadas (mystical inner sounds) are heard very distinctly by the Yogi, because the outside worldly sounds are shut out now. He has deep concentration. Prana, Apana, Nada and Bindu unite now. The Yogi reaches perfection in Yoga.

10. JALANDHARA BANDHA

Contract the throat. Press the chin firmly on the chest. This Bandha is practised at the end of Puraka (inhalation) and beginning of Kumbhaka (retention of breath). By the practice of this Bandha, the Prana moves in the right path. It is united with the Apana. Ida and Pingala Nadis are shut out. The gastric fire which is situated in the region of Nabhi consumes the nectar which exudes out of the Sahasrara through the hole in the palate. The Yogic student should practise this Bandha in order to prevent the nectar being thus consumed. The Yogi drinks the nectar and attains immortality.

11. UDDIYANA BANDHA

Empty the lungs by a strong and forcible exhalation. Now contract and forcibly draw up the intestines and also the navel towards the back, so that the abdomen rests against the back of the body high up in the thoracic cavity. He who practises this Bandha constantly conquers death and becomes young. This helps a lot in keeping up Brahmacharya. All Bandhas awaken the Kundalini. Uddiyana is practised in the end of Kumbhaka and beginning of Rechaka. When you practise this Bandha, the diaphragm, the muscular portion between the thoracic cavity and abdomen, is raised up, the abdominal wall is drawn backwards. Bend your trunk forwards, when you do Uddiyana. Uddiyana can be done in sitting and standing postures. When you practise in the standing posture, place your hand on the knees or a little above the knees. Keep the legs a little apart.

Uddiyana is a blessing to humanity. It imparts beautiful health, strength, vigour and vitality to the practioner.

When it is combined with Nauli Kriya which consists in churning the contents of the abdomen it serves as a powerful gastro-intestinal tonic. These are two potent weapons of the Yogin to combat constipation, weak peristalsis of the intestines and the gastro-intestinal disorders of the alimentary system. It is by these two Yogic exercises alone you can manipulate and massage all the abdominal viscera and tone them up.

Those who want to practise Nauli should practise Uddiyana in the beginning. Uddiyana reduces fat in the belly. For abdominal exercises nothing can compete with Uddiyana and Nauli. They stand unique, unrivalled and unprecedented amongst all systems of physical exercises in the East and the West.

12. YONI MUDRA

Sit in Siddhasana. Close the ears with two thumbs, eyes with the index-fingers, nostrils with the middle fingers, the upper lips with the ring-fingers and the lower lips with the little fingers. This is a beautiful Mudra for doing Japa. Dive deep and meditate on the Shat Chakras and Kundalini. This is not quite easy for all like other Mudras. You have to exert much in getting success in this. You must be perfectly established in Brahmacharya if you want sure success in this Mudra. "*Devanamapi durlabha*"—very difficult to be obtained even by Devas. Therefore realise the importance of this Mudra. Practise it very cautiously.

SECTION SIX

SCIENCE OF PRANAYAMA

There are eight kinds of Kumbhakas which are as follows:

1. Suryabheda
2. Ujjayi
3. Sitkari
4. Sitali
5. Bhastrika
6. Bhramari
7. Murcha
8. Plavini

In some books 'Plavini' is taken as the eighth Kumbhaka. In some other books Kevala Kumbhaka is described as the eighth variety. Though Kapala-Bhati belongs to the Shat-Karmas I have described it here, as it is only a variety of Pranayama exercise.

Prana is the Vayu that moves in the body and its restraint within is known as Kumbhaka. It is of two kinds, viz., Sahita and Kevala. One can hardly obtain perfection in Raja Yoga without Hatha Yoga. At the end of Kumbhaka you should withdraw the mind from all the objects. By gradual and steady practice you will be established in Raja Yoga.

EXERCISE NO. 1

Sit on Padmasana. Close your eyes. Concentrate on Trikuti. Close the right nostril with your right thumb.

Inhale slowly through the left nostril as long as you can do it with comfort. Do not make any sound during inhalation; then exhale slowly. Repeat your Mantra mentally. Do this twelve times. This will constitute one round.

For detailed, complete instructions, refer to my book "Science of Pranayama".

Then inhale through the right nostril by closing the left with your right ring and little fingers. Inhale slowly through the right as before and exhale after closing the left nostril. Do this twelve times.

In the second week of practice do two rounds, in the third week three rounds. Take rest for 5 minutes when one round is over. If you take a few normal breaths when one round is over, that will give you sufficient rest and you will be fresh for the next round. Here there is no Kumbhaka.

EXERCISE NO. 2

Sit on your Asana. Close the right nostril with your right thumb. Then inhale slowly through your left nostril. Close the left nostril with your right ring and little fingers and open the right nostril by removing the right thumb. Exhale slowly through the right nostril.

Then draw the air through the right nostril as long as you can do it with comfort and then exhale through the left nostril by removing the right ring and the little fingers. There is no Kumbhaka in this Pranayama. Repeat the process 12 times. This will constitute one round.

1. KAPALABHATI

This prepares the student for the practice of Bhastrika Pranayama. This is one of the processes known as Shat-Kriyas (six acts) in Hatha Yoga. Those who are well-versed in Kapalabhati can do Bhastrika very easily.

Sit on Padmasana. Keep the hands on the knees. Perform Puraka and Rechaka rapidly like the bellows of a blacksmith. This is called Kapalabhati. This exercise should be performed vigorously. One will get profuse perspiration. There is no Kumbhaka in this practice. Rechaka plays an important part here. Sudden expulsions of breath follow one another in rapid succession. This is a powerful exercise. When it is practised, all tissues, cells, nerves, tendons, molecules will powerfully vibrate.

To start with, you can have a speed of one expulsion per second. Gradually you can increase the speed to two expulsions per second. To begin with, do one round of 'Kapalabhati' in the morning which will consist of ten expulsions only. In the second week do one round in the morning and one round in the evening. In the third week do two rounds in the morning, two rounds in the evening. In the fourth week do three rounds in the morning, three rounds in the evening. Take a little rest when a round is over by taking a few normal breaths. This will relax you quite comfortably. Later on, when you have sufficiently advanced in this practice, increase 10 expulsions for each round till you get 120 expulsions for each round.

This exercise cleanses the skull, the respiratory system and the nasal passages. It destroys diseases of the phlegm. It removes the spasm in bronchial tubes. Consequently asthma is relieved and cured also. The apices of the lungs get abundant supply of oxygen. Thereby they cannot afford favourable nidus for tubercle bacilli (T.B.). Consumption is therefore cured by this practice. Lungs are considerably developed. Carbon dioxide is eliminated on a large scale. Blood is purified. Impurities of the blood are thrown out. Tissues and cells absorb a large quantity of oxygen. Heart functions properly. The circulatory, respiratory and digestive systems are toned to a considerable degree.

2. SURYABHEDA

Sit on Padmasana or Siddhasana, close the eyes. Keep the left nostril closed with your right ring and little fingers. Slowly inhale without making any sound as long as you can do it comfortably through the right nostril. Then retain the breath by resting the chin on the chest. Hold the breath till perspiration oozes from the tips of the nails and the roots of the hairs. This point cannot be reached at the very outset. You will have to increase the period of Kumbhaka gradually. This is the limit of the sphere of practice of Suryabheda. Then exhale very, very slowly without making any sound through the left nostril by closing the right nostril with thumb. Exhale after purifying the skull by forcing the breath up. This destroys the intestinal worms and diseases. This removes the four kinds of evils caused by Vayu and cures Vata (rheumatism). It cures rhinitis of the nose, cephalalgia and various sorts of neuralgia. The worms that are found in the frontal sinuses are removed. It destroys decay and death, awakens the Kundalini Sakti.

3. UJJAYI

Sit on Padmasana or Siddhasana. Close the mouth. Inhale slowly through both the nostrils in a smooth uniform manner till the breath fills the space from the throat to the heart with a noise. Retain the breath as long as you can comfortably do it and then exhale slowly through the left nostril by closing the right nostril with your right thumb. Expand the chest when you inhale. During inhalation a peculiar sound is produced owing to the partial closure of glottis. The sound produced during inhalation should be of a mild and uniform pitch. It should be a continuous sound also. This Kumbhaka may be practised even when walking or standing. Instead of exhaling through the left nostril, you can exhale slowly through both nostrils.

This removes the heat in the head. The practitioner becomes very beautiful. The gastric fire is increased. Asthma, consumption and all sorts of pulmonary diseases are cured. Perform Ujjayi to destroy decay and death.

4. SITKARI

Fold the tongue so that the tip of the tongue might touch the upper palate and draw the air through the mouth with a hissing sound C, C, C, C (Si, Si, Si, Si). Then retain the breath as long as you can without the feeling of suffocation and then exhale slowly through both nostrils. You can keep the two rows of teeth in contact and then inhale the air through the mouth as before. This is a slight modification.

This practice enhances the beauty of the practitioner and the vigour of his body. It removes hunger, thirst, indolence and sleep. When you are thirsty practise this. You will be relieved of thirst immediately.

5. SITALI

Protrude the tongue a little away from the lips. Fold the tongue like a tube. Draw in the air through the mouth with the hissing sound of Si. Retain the breath as long as you can hold on with comfort. Then exhale slowly through nostrils. Practise this daily in the morning for 15 or 30 minutes. You can do this Pranayama either on Padmasana or Siddhasana.

This Pranayama purifies the blood. It quenches thirst and appeases hunger. It cools the system. It destroys Gulma (chronic dyspepsia), Pliha (inflammation of spleen), various chronic skin-diseases, fever, consumption, indigestion, bilious disorder, phlegm and other diseases. Poisons of all sorts in the blood are thrown out. When you are caught in a jungle or any place where you cannot find water, if you feel thirsty, practise this Pranayama. You will be at once relieved of thirst. He who practises this Pranayama will not be affected by the bite of serpents or scorpions.

6. BHASTRIKA

In Sanskrit Bhastrika means bellows. Rapid succession of forcible exhalations is a characteristic feature of Bhastrika. Just as a blacksmith blows his bellows rapidly, so also you should move your breath rapidly. Sit on Padmasana. Keep the body, neck and head erect. Make the palms rest on the knees or laps. Close the mouth. Next inhale and exhale quickly five to ten times like the bellows of a blacksmith. Constantly dilate and contract your lungs. When you practise this Pranayama a hissing sound is produced. The practitioner should start with rapid expulsions of breath following one another in rapid succession. When the required number of expulsions, say ten for a round, is finished, the final expulsion is followed by the deepest possible inhalation. The breath is suspended as long as it can be done with comfort. Then the deepest possible exhalation is done. This deep inhalation completes one round of Bhastrika. Rest a while after one round is over by taking a few easy normal breaths. This will give you relief and make you fit for starting the second round. Do three rounds daily in the morning. You can do three rounds in the evening also. Busy people who find it difficult to do three rounds of Bhastrika daily can do one round only.

This also will keep them quite fit. Bhastrika is a form of powerful exercise. A combination of Kapalabhati and Ujjayi makes up Bhastrika.

Some prolong the practice till they get fatigued. You will get perspiration profusely. If you experience the slightest giddiness stop the practice and take a few normal breaths. Continue the practice after the giddiness has vanished. Bhastrika can be done both in the morning and evening in winter. In summer do it in the morning only during the cool hours.

Bhastrika relieves inflammation of the throat, increases gastric fire, destroys phlegm, removes diseases of the nose and chest and eradicates asthma, consumption, etc. It gives good appetite and breaks the three Granthis or knots, viz., Brahmagranthi, Vishnugranthi and Rudragranthi. It destroys phlegm which is the bolt or obstacle to the door at the mouth of Brahma Nadi (Sushumna). It removes all diseases which arise from excess of wind, bile and phlegm. It gives warmth to the body. When you have no sufficient warm clothing in a cold region to protect yourself from cold, practise this Pranayama and you will get sufficient warmth in the body quickly. It purifies the Nadis considerably. It is the most beneficial of all Kumbhakas. Bhastrika Kumbhaka should be specially practised as it enables the Prana to break through the three Granthis (knots) that are firmly located in the Sushumna. It awakens the Kundalini quickly. The practitioner will always be healthy.

The number of exhalations or rounds is determined by the strength and capacity of the practitioner. You must not go to the extremes. Some students do six rounds. Some do twelve also. Repeat 'Om' mentally with Bhava and meaning throughout the practice. There are some varieties of Bhastrika wherein one nostril only is used for breathing purposes.

Those whole-timed aspirants who want to practise Bhastrika in a serious manner should clean the bowels either through Bhasti or enema in the morning and then start the practice. They should take only Kichidi with plenty of Ghee.

7. BHRAMARI

Sit on Padma or Siddha Asana. Inhale rapidly through both nostrils and exhale rapidly through both nostrils, making the humming sound of a bee.

You can follow the process till the body is bathed in perspiration. In the end inhale through both nostrils, retain the breath as long as you can do it comfortably and then exhale slowly through both nostrils. The joy which the practitioner gets in making the Kumbhaka is unlimited and indescribable. In the beginning, heat of the body is increased as the circulation of blood is quickened and in the end the bodily heat is decreased by perspiration. By success in this Bhramari Kumbhaka, the Yogic student gets success in Samadhi.

8. MURCHA

Sit in your Asana and inhale. Retain the breath. Do Jalandhara Bandha by pressing the chin against the chest. Retain the breath till you expect fainting and then exhale slowly. This is Murcha Kumbhaka as it makes the mind senseless and gives happiness.

9. PLAVINI

Practice of Pranayama demands skill on the part of the students. He who practises this Pranayama can do Jalastambha and float on water for any length of time. Mr. 'S', Yogic student, can float on water for twelve hours at a stretch. He who practises this Plavini Kumbhaka can live on air and dispense with food for some days. The student actually drinks air like water slowly and sends it to the stomach. The stomach gets bloated a bit. If you tap the stomach when it is filled with air you will get a peculiar tympanic (air) sound. Gradual practice is necessary. The help of one who is well-versed in this Pranayama is also necessary. The student can expel all the air from the stomach by gradual belching or by doing Uddiyana Bandha.

10. KEVALA KUMBHAKA

Kumbhaka is of two kinds, viz., Sahita and Kevala. That which is coupled with inhalation and exhalation is termed Sahita. That which is devoid of these is called Kevala (alone). Until you become perfect in Kevala, practise Sahita.

By practice of Kevala Kumbhaka, the knowledge of Kundalini arises. In Kevala Kumbhaka, the breath is suddenly stopped without Puraka and Rechaka. The student can restrain his breath as long as he likes through this Kumbhaka. He obtains the state of Raja Yoga. Through Kevala Kumbhaka the Kundalini is aroused and the Sushumna is free from all sorts of obstacles. He attains perfection in Hatha Yoga. This Kumbhaka cures all diseases and promotes longevity.

You may do this Kumbhaka eight times a day, once in every three hours or five times a day, once in the early morning, then at noon, in the twilight, at midnight, and then in the fourth quarter of the night, or you may do it thrice a day, i.e., in the morning, evening and night.

He who knows Kevala Pranayama is the real Yogi. What can he not accomplish in the three worlds, who has acquired success in this Kevala Kumbhaka? Glory, glory to such exalted souls! May their blessings be upon all Yogic students!

BENEFITS OF PRANAYAMA

Through Pranayama the body becomes strong and healthy. Too much fat is reduced. There is a lustre in the face. Eyes sparkle like diamonds. The practitioner becomes very handsome. Voice becomes sweet and melodious. The inner Anahata sounds are distinctly heard. The student is free from all sorts of diseases. He fully gets established in Brahmacharya. The Jatharagni is augmented. Appetite becomes keen. Nadis are purified. The mind becomes one-pointed, Ekagra. Rajas and Tamas are destroyed. The mind is prepared for Dharana and Dhyana. The excretions become scanty.

Steady practice of Pranayama arouses the inner spiritual force and brings in ecstatic joy, spiritual light and peace of mind. The student becomes so perfected in Brahmacharya that his mind will be unshaken even if a fairy tries to entice him. It makes him an Urdhvareto-Yogi. An advanced Yogi acquires the major Ashta Siddhis, Anima, Mahima, Garima, etc., and 36 minor Siddhis.

If you practise Asanas and Pranayamas without Brahmacharya and dietetic regulations, even for a long period, you will not get much benefit. For ordinary health, you can practise only a little of Pranayama.

HINTS ON PRANAYAMA

1. Practise Pranayama in a dry, well-ventilated room. Remain alone in the room during the practice.

2. Get up at 4 a.m. Meditate or do Japa for half an hour. Then do Asanas. Take rest for 20 to 30 minutes. Then do physical exercises. Again take a little rest. Then practise Pranayama. Physical exercises can be harmoniously combined with Asanas. Have two sittings in morning and evening. Pranayama can be practised just before you sit for Japa or meditation. It will make your body light and you will enjoy your meditation.

3. Do not practise Pranayama when the stomach is loaded. The stomach must be empty or light during practice. Take a small cup of milk 10 minutes after the practice.

4. Take Sattvic food, such as milk, fruits, green Dhal, Parota (bread), Lauki (vegetable). Give up hot curries and chutnies, chillies, oil, onions, garlic, meat, fish, alcohol and smoking.

5. Be regular and systematic in your practice. Never miss a day.

6. Do not take bath immediately after Pranayama. Take rest for half an hour.

7. Do not wipe the perspiration with a towel. Rub with your hands. Do not expose the body to chill draughts of air when you perspire.

8. Have one sitting only in the morning during summer. If there is heat in the brain or head apply Amala oil or butter on the head before you take bath. Take Misri Sharbat by dissolving sugar-candy in water. This will cool your whole system.

9. Do Sitali Pranayama also. You will not be affected by the heat.

10. Perfect celibacy for six months or one year will

doubtless enables you to acquire rapid progress in the practice and in spiritual advancement. Do not talk with ladies. Do not laugh and joke with them. Shun their company entirely during this period at least.

11. Always inhale and exhale very, very slowly. Do not make any sound when you inhale and exhale. In Kapalabhati and Bhastrika do not produce violent sound.

12. Do not perform Pranayama when you are fatigued. There must always be joy and exhilaration of spirit during and after the practice. You should come out of the practice fully invigorated and refreshed. Do not bind your self by many rules (Niyamas).

13. Strictly avoid too much talking, eating, sleeping mixing with friends and exertion.

14. Gradually increase the period of Kumbhaka. Retain for 4 seconds in the first week, for 8 seconds in the second week, for 12 seconds in the third week, and so on, till you are able to retain the breath for 64 seconds.

15. Repeat Om or Gayatri mentally during Puraka Kumbhaka and Rechaka. Have the feeling (Bhava) that all Daivic Sampats such as mercy, forgiveness, love, etc., enter your system during inhalation and all Asuric qualities such as lust, anger, greed, etc., are thrown out during exhalation. Also feel when you inhale that you draw energy from the Divine Source—cosmic Prana—and that your whole body from top to toe is saturated with abundant fresh energy. Stop the practice when you are seriously ailing.

16. A neophyte should do Puraka and Rechaka only without any Kumbhaka for some days.

17. You must so nicely adjust the Puraka, Kumbhaka and Rechaka that you should not experience the feeling of suffocation or discomfort at any stage of Pranayamas.

18. You need not unnecessarily prolong the period of exhalation. If you prolong the time Rechaka, the following

inhalation will be done in a hurried manner and rhythm will be broken.

19. You must so carefully regulate the Puraka, Kumbhaka and Rechaka that you must be able to do with absolute comfort and care, not only one Pranayama, but the full course or required rounds of Pranayama. You have to repeat this often. Experience and practice will make you all right. Be steady.

20. You should never feel the necessity of catching hold of a few normal breaths between any two successive rounds. The duration of Puraka, Kumbhaka and Rechaka must be properly kept up. Exercise due care and attention. Matters will turn out to be successful and easy.

21. Another important point is that you must have efficient control over the lungs at the end of Kumbhaka to enable you to do the Rechaka smoothly and in proportion with the Puraka.

22. Have the ratio 1:4:2 for Puraka, Kumbhaka and Rechaka. Inhale till you count 1 Om, retain the breath for 4 Oms, and exhale it for 2 Oms. Every week increase the ratio 2:8:4. 3:12:6 and so on, till you get the maximum ratio of 16:64:32. Use the fingers of your left hand for counting Om. The ratio comes by itself when you inhale, retain and exhale as long as you can do it comfortably. When you have advanced in practice you need not count. You will be naturally established in the normal ratio through the force of habit.

23. Slight errors may crop up in the beginning. It does not matter. Do not be unnecessarily alarmed. Do not give up the practice. You will learn yourself how to adjust the three processes of Puraka, Kumbhaka and Rechaka nicely. Common-sense, instinct, shrill inner voice of the soul will help you in the path. Everything will come out smoothly in the end. Start the practice this very second in

right earnest and become a real Yogi. Strive, struggle hard and attain the goal.

24. Suryabheda and Ujjayi produce heat. Sitkari and Sitali are cooling. Bhastrika preserves normal temperature. Suryabheda destroys the excess of wind, Ujjayi, phlegm, Sitkari and Sitali bile, and Bhastrika all the three.

25. Suryabheda and Ujjayi must be practised in winter. Sitkari and Sitali must be practised during summer. Bhastrika can be practised in all the seasons. Those persons whose bodies are hot even in winter can practise Sitali and Sitkari in winter.

NOTE:—Many of the instructions given for "Asanas," are to be observed for Pranayama also.

YOGA ADDENDA

KUNDALINI

Kundalini is the coiled up sleeping Divine Sakti that lies dormant in all beings. Two digits above the anus (Guda) and two digits below the organ of generation is the Muladhara Chakra. Here lies the Supreme Goddess Kundalini. It has three and a half coils like a serpent. Hence it is styled as "Serpent Power." It is in the mouth of Sushumna Nadi with face downwards. It represents the creative force of the world and is always engaged in creation. The three coils represent the three Gunas of Prakriti, viz., Sattva, Rajas and Tamas. The half coil represents the Vikritis, the modifications of the Prakriti. The rousing of Kundalini Sakti and its union with Siva in Sahasrara Chakra effect the state of Samadhi and liberation. The Yogi will possess 8 major and 32 minor Siddhis. He can live as long as he likes.

IDA, PINGALA, SUSHUMNA AND SHAT-CHAKRAS

The Nadis, Ida and Pingala, cross the central column from one side to the other and make a threefold knot with the Sushumna, called Triveni.

Ida flows through the left nostril and Pingala runs through the right nostril. Sushumna is the most important Nadi. It is known as Brahma Nadi. This is a fine channel that runs along the centre of the spinal cord from the base, Muladhara Chakra, up to Brahmarandhra. When the Chakras have been purified by a regular course of Pranayama, the breath easily forces itself into the mouth of Sushumna Nadi and enters it. When the breath flows through Sushumna, the mind becomes steady.

As for the detailed instructions and functions of these Nadis and Chakras, refer to my book "Kundalini Yoga".

ABHYASA-KRAMA AND DINACHARYA

ELEMENTARY COURSE "A" FOR BUSY PEOPLE

	Duration	*From*	*To*
Japa and Meditation	0-45	4.00 a.m.	4-45 a.m.
Sirshasana	0- 5		
Sarvangasana	0- 5		
Matsyasana	0- 3		
Paschimottanasana	0- 5	} 4.45 a.m.	5.10 a.m.
Other Asanas	0- 5		
Savasana	0- 2		
Rest	0-15	5.10 a.m.	5.25 a.m.
Bhastrika Pranayama & Other Pranayamas	0-10	5.25 a.m.	5.35 a.m.
Rest	0- 5	5.35 a.m.	5.40 a.m.
Study (Svadhyaya)	0-45	5.40 a.m.	6.25 a.m.
Morning Walk	0-35	6.25 a.m.	7.00 a.m.
Asanas, Pranayama, Japa and Meditation (reverse order)	1-30	6.15 p.m.	7.45 p.m.
Bhajan (Kirtan)	0-30	7.45 p.m.	8.15 p.m.
Meals and Rest	0-15	8.15 p.m.	8.30 p.m.
Study	1-00	8.30 p.m.	9.30 p.m.
Sleep	6-00	9.30 p.m.	3.30 p.m.

ADVANCED COURSE "B" FOR BUSY PEOPLE

Japa and Meditation	1-30	3.30 a.m.	5.00 a.m.
Sirshasana	0-30	5.00 a.m.	5.30 a.m.
Sarvangasana, Matsyasana, Paschimottanasana etc.	0-30	5.30 a.m.	6.00 a.m.
Bhastrika and the other Pranayamas	0-30	6.00 a.m.	6.30 a.m.
Study (Svadhyaya)	0-30	6.30 a.m.	7.00 a.m.
Asanas, Pranayama, Japa and Meditation	3-00	6.15 p.m.	9.15 p.m.
Meals	0-15	9.15 p.m.	9.30 p.m.
Study	0-30	9.30 p.m.	10.00 p.m.
Sleep	5-00	10.00 p.m.	3.00 a.m.

COURSE "C" FOR WHOLE-TIMED ASPIRANTS

Japa and Meditation	3-30	3.30 a.m.	7.00 a.m.
Asanas and Pranayama	2-00	7.00 a.m.	9.00 a.m.
Asanas and Pranayama	2-00	5.00 p.m.	7.00 p.m.
Japa and Meditation	2-00	7.00 p.m.	9.00 p.m.
Bhajan	1-00	9.00 p.m.	10.00 p.m.
Sleep	5-00	10.00 p.m.	3.30 a.m.

COMMON ROUTINE FOR "A" & "B" COURSES

Rest, Chota Hazri or a cup of Milk	0-15	7.00 a.m.	7.15 a.m.
Nishkama Karma and Household Duties	1-15	7.15 a.m.	8.30 a.m.
Bathing, washing, breakfast, etc.	1-00	8.30 a.m.	9.30 a.m.
Office	3-00	10.00 a.m.	1.00 p.m.
Lunch, Writing Letters and Interviews	1-00	1.00 p.m.	2.00 p.m.
Office	3-00	2.00 p.m.	5.00 p.m.
Evening Tiffin and Rest	0-15	5.00 p.m.	5.15 p.m.
Evening Walk 2 Miles, Satsanga Sravana	1-15	5.15 p.m.	6.30 p.m.

During other times, Mouna, Nishkama Karma, Kirtan, Study, Bath, Meals, etc., must be nicely arranged. Aspirants should have their own routine according to their growth, capacity and convenience.

IMPORTANT HINTS

1. Every aspirant in Yoga should have a similar routine. You can make a few changes in time here and there; but every item of the routine should be there. Mere Vedantic gossiping will not do in the spiritual path. You must be very strict in observing punctuality and every item of the routine should be carried out at any cost. The time given for meditation, Japa, Asana and Pranayama should be gradually increased.

2. As soon as you get up from bed, evacuate your bowels first; wash your hands, legs and face if you cannot take bath; and then sit for meditation and other Yogic practices.

3. After regular practice for some days, if you increase the period of doing Asanas, Pranayama and meditation, you will have to curtail the item that is allotted to household duties and morning walk. On holidays more time should be utilised for the spiritual practices.

4. During the period of the morning 'study', you should read the Gita, the Upanishads, the Ramayana, etc., and in the night 'study', you can read some other philosophical books or journals. These two items are something like the detailed and non-detailed texts of the students. You can utilise the time of interview and writing letters, in studying some interesting books.

5. In the evening you can profitably combine other physical exercises and a few rounds of Pranayama. While you practise Pranayama and during other works also, do Japa mentally.

6. When you perform Kirtan in the night, include the members of your family, friends, neighbours and servants also. In the end distribute Prasad.

7. Under the heading Nishkama Karma, treatment or

nursing of the sick is the best. If you cannot do this, give private tuition to the poor students or do charity.

8. Due to unavoidable circumstances if you cannot attend to any item of the routine, that time should be utilised for Mouna, study or gardening. The mind must be kept busy always in doing similar useful works.

9. In the short course 'A', Asanas and Pranayama can be done first and then Japa and Meditation. In the advanced course 'B', Asanas and Pranayama should be practised after Japa and Meditation, as the morning time (Brahmamuhurta) is the best for Meditation. To drive away drowsiness, you can practise Sirshasana or Bhastrika for about 10 minutes before starting Japa and Meditation.

10. If you fail to do any one of the items, dear brother, please note that you have killed a day in your precious life. In case you find any disturbing elements in the world, mercilessly, without any hesitation, renounce the world and take to seclusion and devote day and night to Spiritual Sadhana at the Lotus-Feet of your Guru. If you are steady, earnest and sincere, in six months' time you will find an inexpressible joy, mental peace and unalloyed bliss. There will be Jyotis in your very face. Such a man is really a blessing for the whole world. This kind of Sadhana alone can give you eternal satisfaction and happiness. You will have to repent in your old age if you depend for your happiness on a few ginger biscuits, a little money and a woman.

YOGA ASANAS

(EXHAUSTIVE LIST OF ASANAS)

1. Ardha Salabhasana
2. Ardha Dhanurasana
3. Ardha Pavanamuktasana
4. Ardha Bhuja Pidasana
5. Akarshana Dhanurasana
6. Ardha Matsyendrasana
7. Ardha Trikonasana
8. Ardha Padasana
9. Ardha Mandukasana
10. Ananda Mandirasana
11. Ardha Padmasana
12. Ardha Kurmasana
13. Ardha Vrikshasana
14. Abhanasana
15. Angushthasana
16. Ardhasana
17. Arpakasana
18. Ardha Savasana
19. Ardha Vrischikasana
20. Adhomukha Savasana
21. Ardha Chandrasana
22. Ardha Padma Paschimottanasana
23. Ardha Navasana
24. Adhvasana
25. Balameru Dandasana
26. Buddhasana
27. Bakasana

28. Bhujangasana
29. Bhrishtasana
30. Bhrishta Valitarikshasana
31. Bhadrasana
32. Bhujasana
33. Bhairavasana
34. Chakrasana
35. Chasangasana
36. Chatushpadasana
37. Chitta Vivekasana
38. Chittasana
39. Chaturmukha Konasana
40. Chatusthambhasana
41. Chakorasana
42. Dhanurasana
43. Durvasasana
44. Dardurasana
45. Dakshina Sakhasana
46. Dakshina Pada Sirshasana
47. Dakshina Janvasana
48. Dakshina Hasta Chatushkonasana
49. Dakshinardhapadasana
50. Dadhi Manthasana
51. Dakshina Hasta Bhayankarasana
52. Dakshina Svasa Kamanasana
53. Dakshina Padasana
54. Dakshina Sananiyasana
55. Dvipada Sirshasana
56. Dakshinardha Pada Padmasana
57. Dakshina Dhirasana

58. Dakshina Pada Abhanasana
59. Dakshina Vakrasana
60. Dandasana
61. Dhirudasana
62. Dvipada Parsvasana
63. Dakshina Pada Paschimottanasana
64. Dhirasana
65. Dakshinangushthasana
66. Dakshina Bhujasana
67. Dakshina Siddhasana
68. Dakshina Trikonasana
69. Dakshina Tarkasana
70. Dakshinasana
71. Eka Pada Vrikshasana
72. Eka Hasta Mayurasana
73. Eka Hasta Bhujasana
74. Eka Padasana
75. Gandabherundasana
76. Gomukhasana
77. Garbhasana
78. Garudasana
79. Gomukha Paschimottanasana
80. Granthi Pidasana
81. Gorakshasana
82. Guptasana
83. Hridaya Kamalasana
84. Hridaya Kamala Muktasana
85. Hasta Parsva Chalanasana
86. Hasta Bhujasana
87. Hasta Pada Sirshasana

88. Hasta Pada Angushthasana
89. Halasana
90. Hamsasana
91. Hanumanasana
92. Hasta Bhayankarasana
93. Hasta Chatushkonasana
94. Hastasana
95. Janusirshasana
96. Janu Parsvasana
97. Jesthikasana
98. Janvasana
99. Krishnasana
100. Kukkutasana
101. Karna Prishtha Janu Padmasana
102. Kasyapasana
103. Kattirikolasana
104. Kurmasana
105. Kamadahanasana
106. Kapilasana
107. Kapalasana
108. Karnapidasana
109. Karmukasana
110. Kesaryasana
111. Kshemasana
112. Kandapidasana
113. Kashtasana
114. Kubjikasana
115. Kshemakonasana
116. Lolasana
117. Loulyasana

118. Marichasana
119. Mayurasana
120. Matsyasana
121. Matsyendrasana
122. Matanda Padmasana
123. Mendakasana
124. Mushti Parsva Bhunamanasana
125. Mushtyasana
126. Makarasana
127. Mukta Hasta Sirshasana
128. Maha Meghasana
129. Matsyendra Siddhasana
130. Matsyendra Padmasana
131. Markatasana
132. Mritasana
133. Mukta Padmasana
134. Mukta Hasta Vrikshasana
135. Muktasana
136. Navasana
137. Nagasana
138. Nisvasasana
139. Natarajasana
140. Niralamba Sirshasana
141. Nischalasana
142. Nishta Asana
143. Nasika Prishthasana
144. Namaskarasana
145. Urdhva Sammukta Padmasana
146. Urdhva Padmasana
147. Urdhva Sarvangasana

148. Urdhva Sammuktasana
149. Urdhva Trikonasana
150. Urdhva Kattirikolasana
151. Urdhva Sirsha Ekapada Chakrasana
152. Urdhva Hasta Janu Balasana
153. Urdhva Mukta Svasanasana
154. Urdhva Padmasana
155. Urdhva Sirshasana
156. Urdhva Dhanurasana
157. Urdhva Bhujangasana
158. Urdhva Paschimottanasana
159. Omkarasana
160. Parsva Bhu Namasana
161. Parsva Valita Vrikshasana
162. Parisarita Pada Vyutthanasana
163. Pada Konasana
164. Baddha Yonyasana
165. Proudhasana
166. Putasana
167. Paryankasana
168. Pada Pidasana
169. Proudha Padasana
170. Purna Padasana
171. Purna Dhanasana
172. Prishtha Hasta Dandasana
173. Pada Vrikshasana
174. Palayanasana
175. Padmasana
176. Purva Trikasana
177. Prishtaskandasana

178. Purna Pada Trikonasana
179. Paschimottanasana
180. Parvatasana
181. Pada Padmasana
182. Padangushthasana
183. Pada Janusirshasana
184. Pranasana
185. Pada Hastasana
186. Prarthanasana
187. Parivartana Padasana
188. Purna Hasta Bhujasana
189. Phanindrasana
190. Padma Mayurasana
191. Rishikasana
192. Sukhasana
193. Svastikasana
194. Salabhasana
195. Suptotthita Pada Janusirshasana
196. Suptotthita Parivartana Padasana
197. Sampurna Bhujasana
198. Sarvangasana
199. Sarvanga Halasana
200 Sarvanga Padmasana
201. Sirshasana
202. Savasana
203. Sirsha Pada Hasta Konasana
204. Sarvatobhadrasana
205. Supta Parsva Padangushthasana
206. Supta Konasana
207. Supta Vajrasana

208. Skandasana
209. Saashtangasana
210. Sthirasana
211. Svasanasana
212. Simhasana
213. Sankatasana
214. Sarva Sangasana
215. Sobhasirayasana
216. Sundasana
217. Sirsha Baddha Hasta Trikonasana
218. Salamba Sirshasana
219. Saakhasana
220. Samanasana
221. Trivikranamasana
222. Tiryaksthambhanasana
223. Tittibhasana
224. Tarkasana
225. Tolangulasana
226. Trikonasana
227. Tiryakmukha Vyutthanasana
228. Trisulasana
229. Tadasana
230. Utthitasana
231. Upavishta Konasana
232. Utthita Parsva Konasana
233. Ugrasana
234. Utthana Padasana
235. Utthana Mandukasana
236. Upavishta Sirshasana
237. Utthita Vivekasana

238. Utthita Samakonasana
239. Uttamangasana
240. Vistrita Pada Parsva Bhu Namasana
241. Vallariyasana
242. Vichasavasana
243. Vipattanasana
244. Vama Svasa Kamanasana
245. Vama Pada Dhirasana
246. Vama Sakasana
247. Vama Pada Abhanasana
248. Vamangushthasana
249. Vama Vakrasana
250. Vama Chananiyasana
251. Vama Prishtha Janu Vrikshasana
252. Vamardha Padasana
253. Vama Pidasana
254. Vamardha Padmasana
255. Vetalasana
256. Vyutthita Hasta Padmasana
257. Vyutkatasana
258. Vajrasana
259. Viparita Dandasana
260. Viparita Dhanurasana
261. Vatayanasana
262. Vrischikasana
263. Virya Stambhanasana
264. Vivekasana
265. Vishnullasana
266. Vamapada Pavanamuktasana
267. Vama Hasta Bhayankarasana

268. Vamahasta Bhujasana
269. Vama Trikonasana
270. Vama Tarkasana
271. Vamanasana
272. Vibhakta Janusirshasana
273. Viramasana
274. Yoga Dandasana
275. Yoga Nidrasana
276. Yoni Asana
277. Yogasana

GLOSSARY

ALASYA—Laziness.

Anahata Sound—Mystical inner sound.

Anahata Chakra—Cardiac plexus, lotus of the heart.

Ananda—Bliss, happiness, joy.

Anga—Limb, step.

Antahkarana—The fourfold internal organs, Manas, Buddhi, Chitta and Ahamkara.

Asana—Pose, posture.

Asana Jaya—Mastery over Asana.

Asuric—Devilish.

Avarana—Veil of ignorance.

BHAVANA—Feeling.

Bhrukuti—The space between the eyebrows.

Bhrumadhya Drishti—Gazing at the Bhrukuti.

Brahmachari—Celibate.

Brahmacharya—Celibacy.

CHAKRA—Plexus.

DAIVI SAMPAT—Divine qualities.

Deha Adhyasa—Attachment to the body.

Dharana—Concentration.

Dvesha—Repulsion.

EKAGRATA—One-pointedness of mind, concentration.

GUDA—Anus.

Gulma—Chronic gastritis.

HRIDAYA GRANTHI—Heart-knot of ignorance.

Humours—Wind, bile and phlegm.

INDRIYAS—Sense-organs.

JADA—Insentient.

Jalodara—Dropsy.

Japa—Repetition of Mantra or God's name.

Jatharagni—Digestive fire.

Jyotis—Illumination.

KUMBHAKA—Retention of breath.

LANGOTI—Loin Cloth.

MALA—Impurities.

Meru Danda—Spinal column.

Misri—Sugar-candy.

Mitahara—Moderation in diet.

Moksha—Liberation, salvation.

Mukti—Final emancipation.

NABHI—Navel.

Nadis—Nerves.

Nadi Suddhi—Purification of Nadis.

Nasikagra Drishti—Gazing at the tip of the nose.

Nididhyasana—Profound meditation.

Nishkama Karma—Action without any expectation of fruits.

Niyama—The second step of Raja Yoga. Internal and external purification, contentment, austerity, study, worship of God, etc.

OJAS-SAKTI—Seminal energy.

PLIHA—Inflammation of the spleen.

Puraka—Inhalation.

RAGA—Attraction.

Rajas—Passion.

Rechaka—Exhalation.

SADHAKA—Aspirant, a practitioner.

Sadhana—Spiritual practice.

Sakti—Power.

Samadhi—Superconscious state, God-consciousness.

Samskaras—Impressions of sense-objects.

Santosha—Contentment.

Satsanga—Association with the wise.

Sattva—Purity.

Siddha—Perfected Yogi.

Siddhi—Perfection, psychic powers.

Sthirata—Firmness, steadiness.

Svabhava—One's own nature.

Svadhyaya—Study of religious books.

TAMAS—Inertia, darkness.

Trikuti—The space between the eyebrows.

UPASANA—Worship.

VAIRAGYA—Dispassion.

Vasana—Impulse, subtle form of desire.

Vikshepa—Tossing of mind.

Viveka—Discrimination between the real and the unreal.

Vritti—Mental modification.

YAMA—The first step of Raja Yoga. Non-killing, truthfulness, non-stealing, continence, non-appropriation, etc.

Yukti—Common-sense, logic.

SURYA NAMASKARA

IN 12 POSTURES

POSTURE 1 (P. 3)

POSTURE 2 (P. 3)

POSTURE 3 (P. 4)

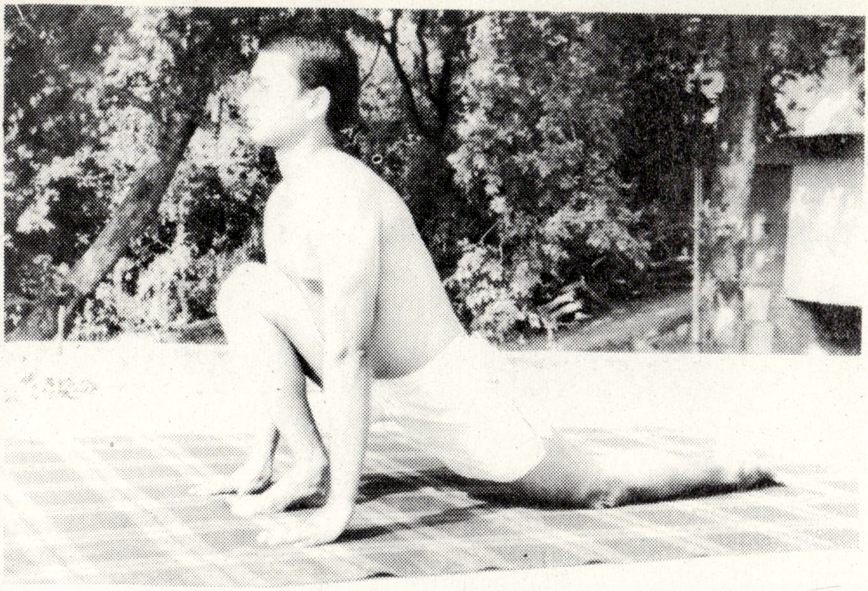

POSTURE 4 (P. 4)

POSTURE 5 (P. 4)

POSTURE 6 (P. 4)

POSTURE 7 (P. 4)

POSTURE 8 (P. 4)

POSTURE 9 (P. 4)

POSTURE 10 (P. 4)

POSTURE 11 (P. 4)

POSTURE 12 (P. 4)

YOGA ASANAS

PADMASANA (P. 8)

SIDDHASANA
(P. 10)

SVASTIKASANA (P. 12)

SUKHASANA (P. 12)

SUKHASANA (*Variation*)

SIRSHASANA (*Front View*) (P. 14)

SIRSHASANA (*Side View*)

SARVANGASANA

(P. 17)

HALASANA (P. 20)

MATSYASANA (P. 21)

PASCHIMOTTANASANA (P. 23)

MAYURASANA (P. 24)

LOLASANA (P. 26)

ARDHAMATSYENDRASANA
(*Front View*) (P. 27)

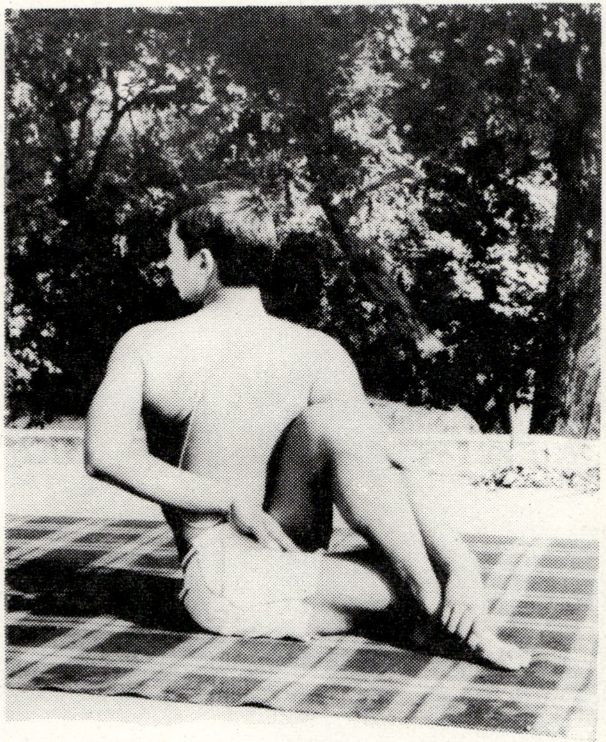

ARDHAMATSYENDRASANA
(*Back View*)

SALABHASANA

(P. 28)

PURNA SALABHASANA

BHUJANGASANA (P. 30)

DHAṄURASANA (P. 31)

AKARSHANA DHANURASANA (P. 32)

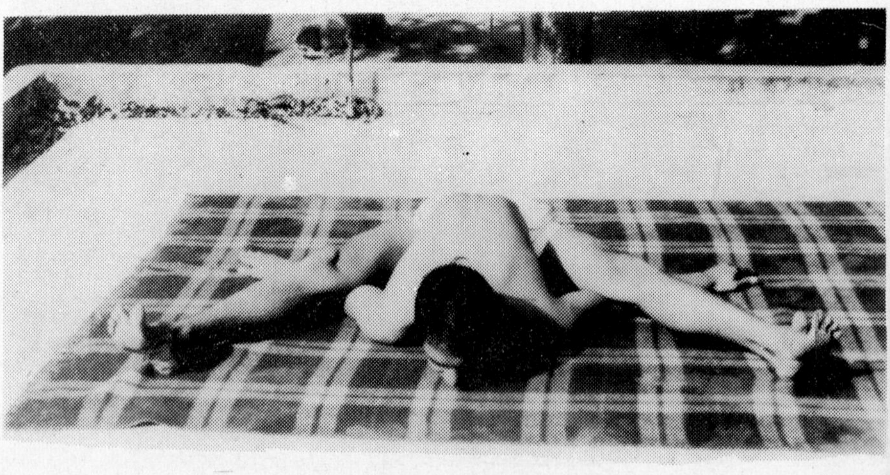

KURMASANA (P. 35)

VAJRASANA (P. 34)
(*Front View*)

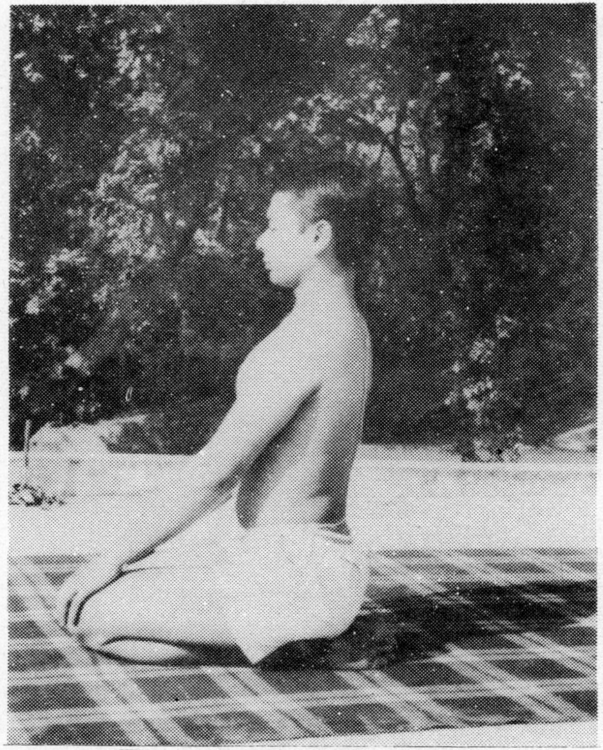

VAJRASANA
(*Side View*)

GOMUKHASANA (P. 33)
(Front View)

GOMUKHASANA
(Side View)

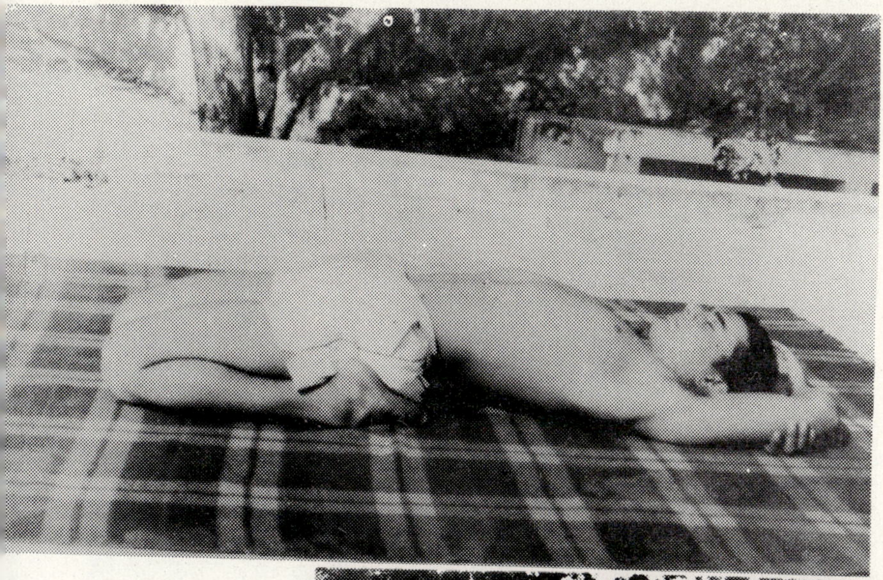

SUPTA VAJRASANA

(P. 36)

GARUDASANA

(P. 37)

URDHVA PADMASANA (P. 38)

PADANGUSHTHASANA (P. 39)

TRIKONASANA (P. 40)

TRIKONASANA (*Variation*)

BADDHA PADMASANA (P. 41)
(*Front View*)

BADDHA PADMASANA
(*Back View*)

PADA HASTASANA (P. 43)

CHAKRASANA (P. 47)

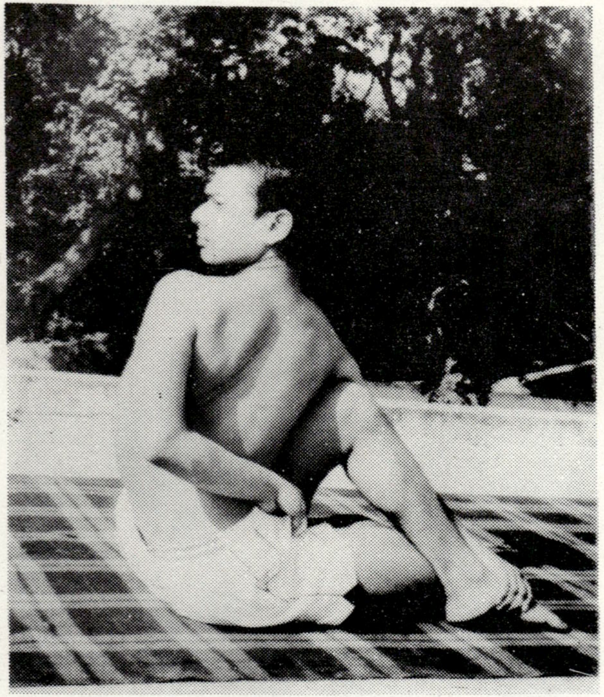

ARDHA MATSYENDRASANA (P. 27)

PURNA MATSYENDRASANA

SAVASANA
(P. 48)

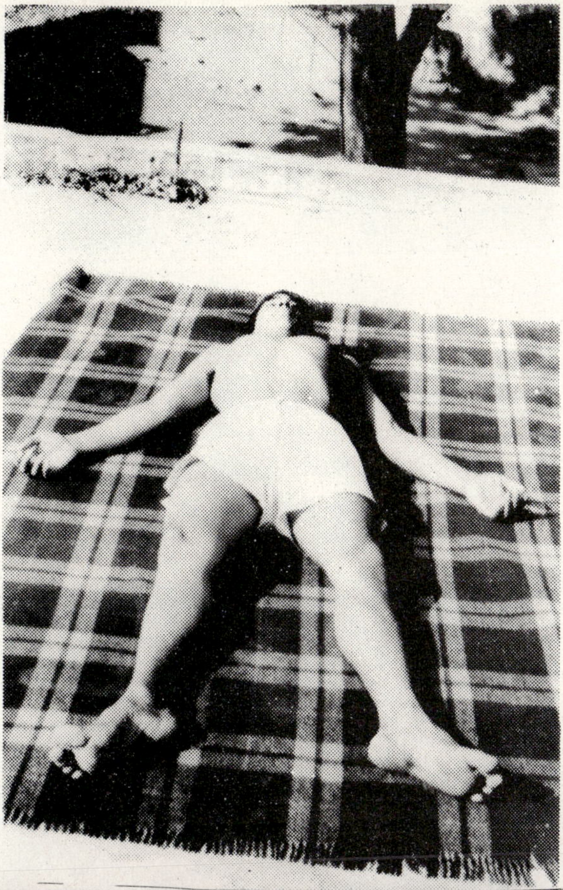

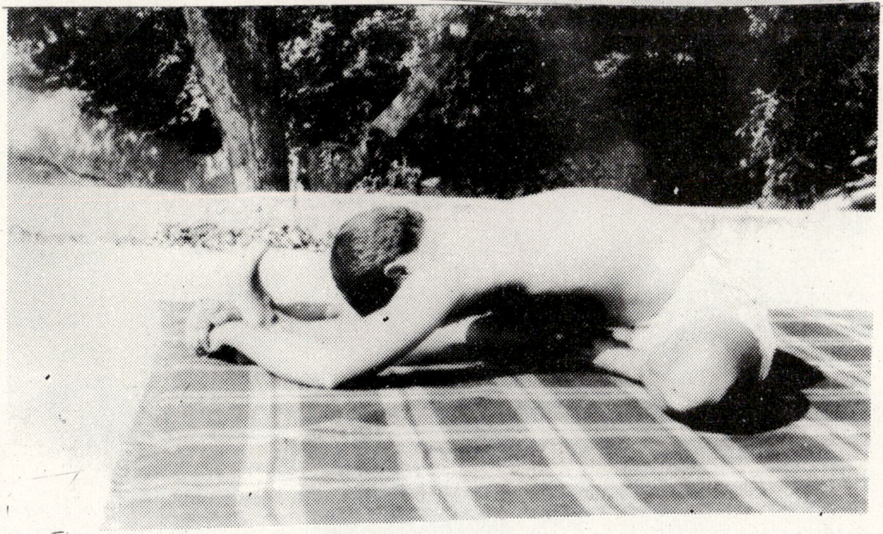

JANUSIRSHASANA (P. 50)

TOLANGULASANA

(P. 51)

GARBHASANA
(P. 51)

SASANGASANA

(P. 52)

SANKATASANA

(P. 54)

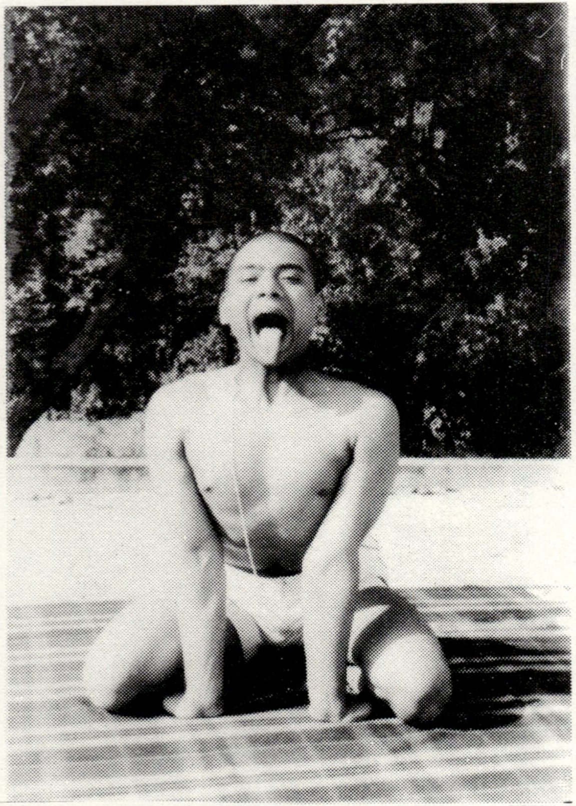

SIMHASANA (P. 52)
(*Front View*)

SIMHASANA
(*Side View*)

KANDAPIDASANA
(P. 53)

KANDAPIDASANA (*Variation*)

YOGASANA (P. 54)

UTKATASANA (P. 55)

JESHTHIKASANA (P. 55)

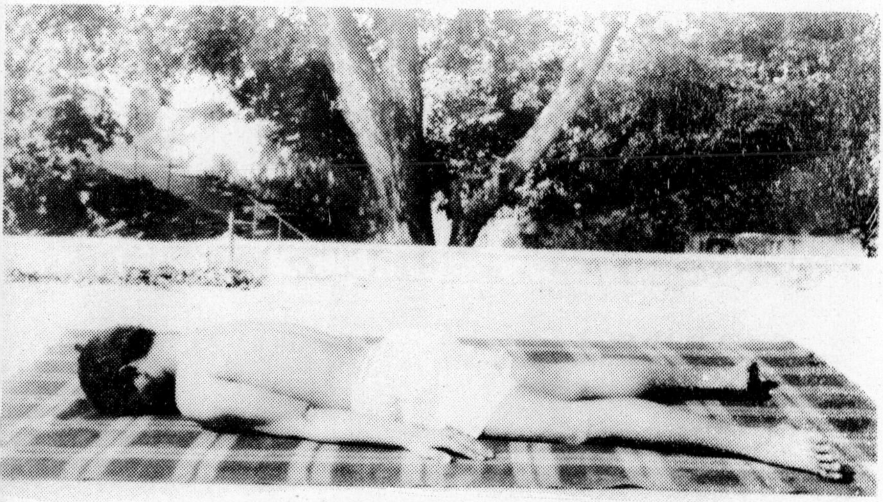

ADHVASANA (P. 56)

USHTRASANA
(P. 56)

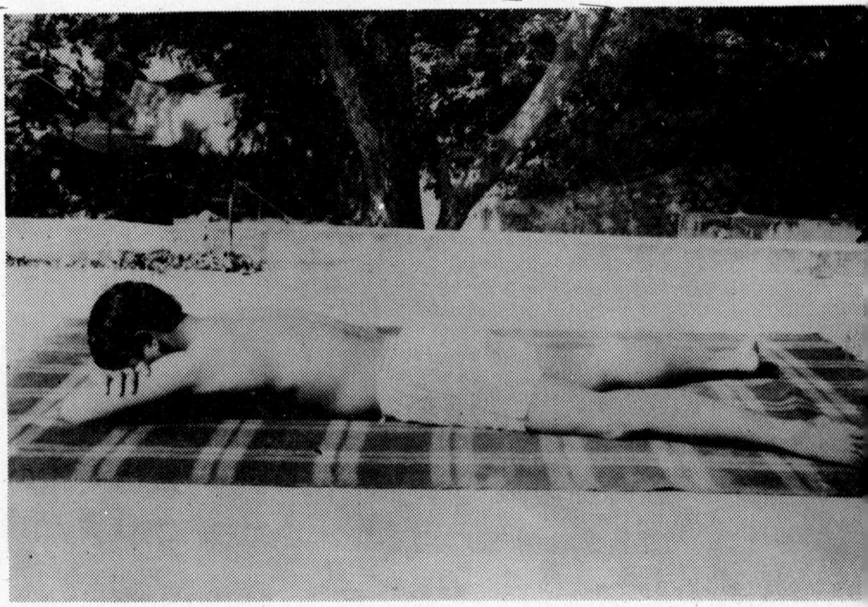

MAKARASANA (P. 56)

VRISCHIKASANA (P. 56)

VRISCHIKASANA (*Variation*)

HASTA
VRISCHIKASANA

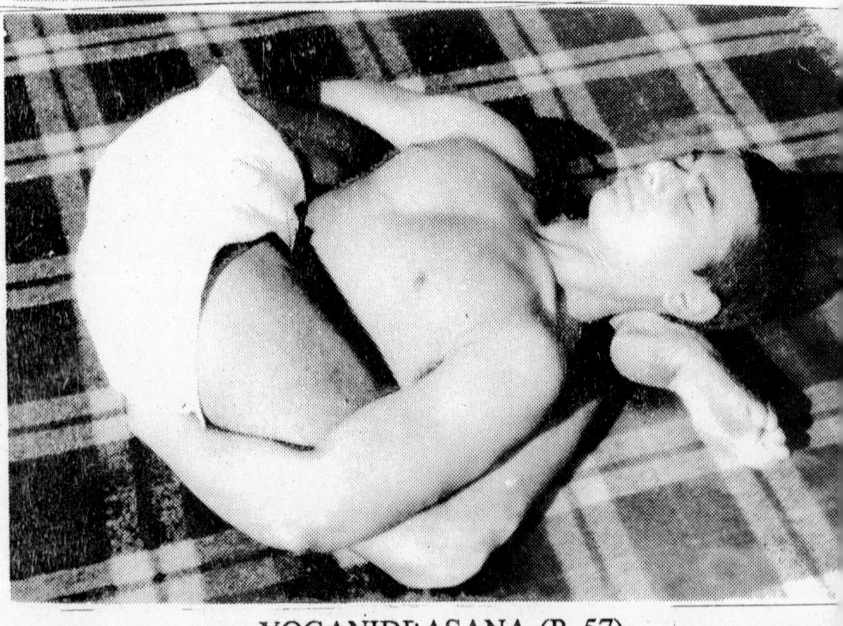

YOGANIDRASANA (P. 57)

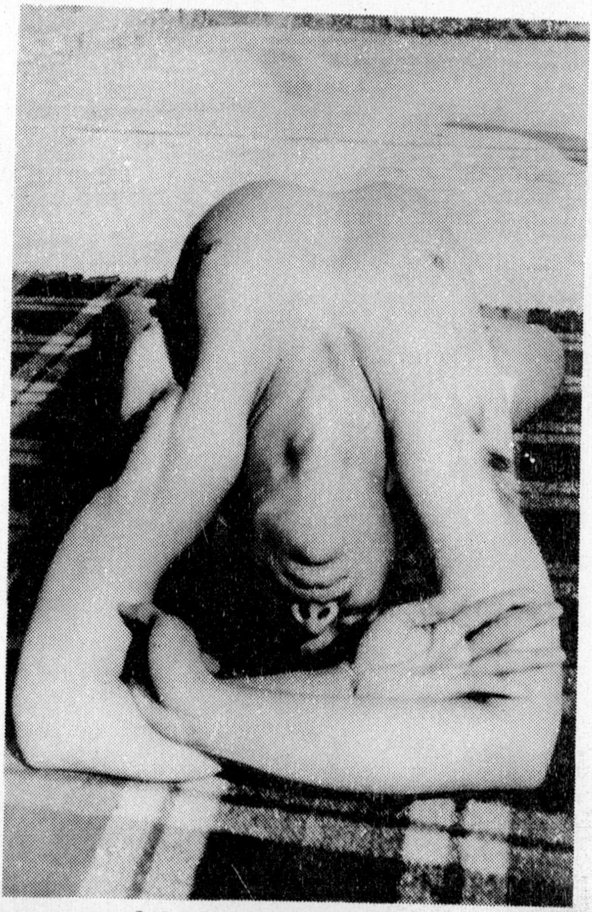

ARYAKASANA
(*Front View*)
(P. 58)

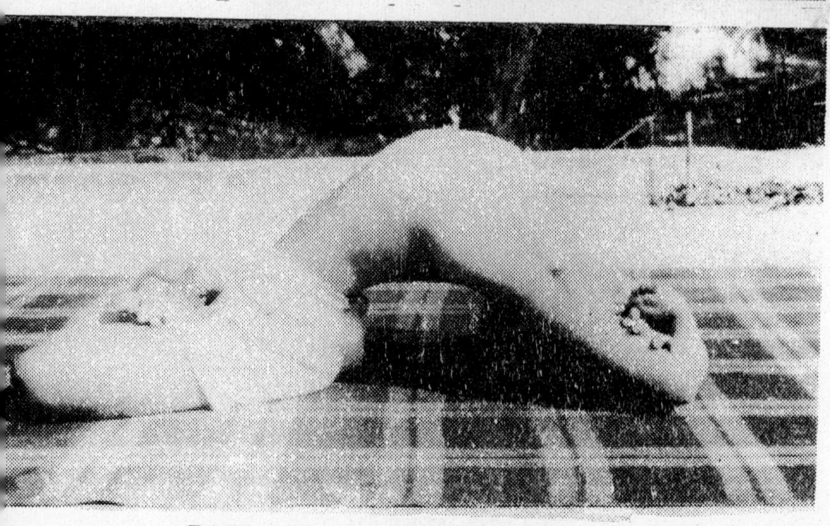

PARYANKASANA (*Side View*)

VATAYANASANA
(P. 58)

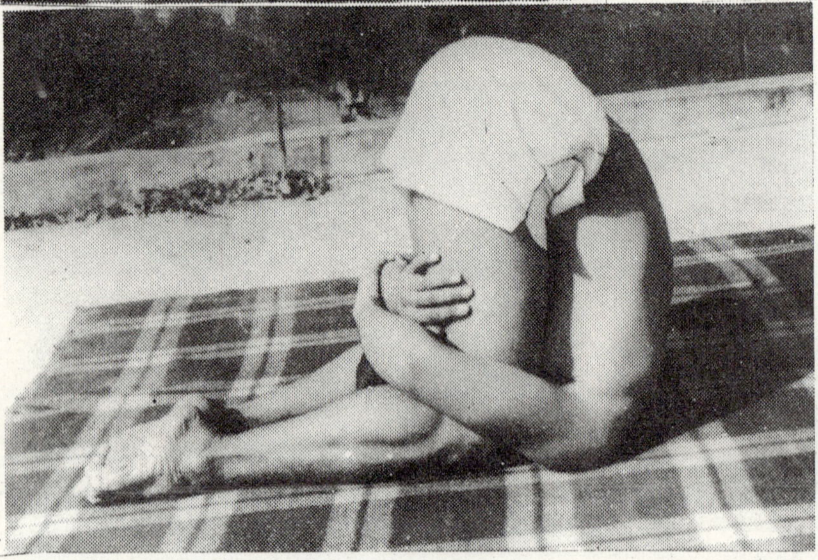

KARNAPIDASANA (P. 57)

NATARAJASANA

BRHMACHARYASANA

OMKARASANA

HANUMANASANA

HASTA
VRIKSHASANA
(P. 17)

RAJAHAMSASANA

DVIPADASIRASANA

BAKASANA

KUKKUTASANA (P. 53)

EKAPADASIRSHASANA

BHAIRAVASANA

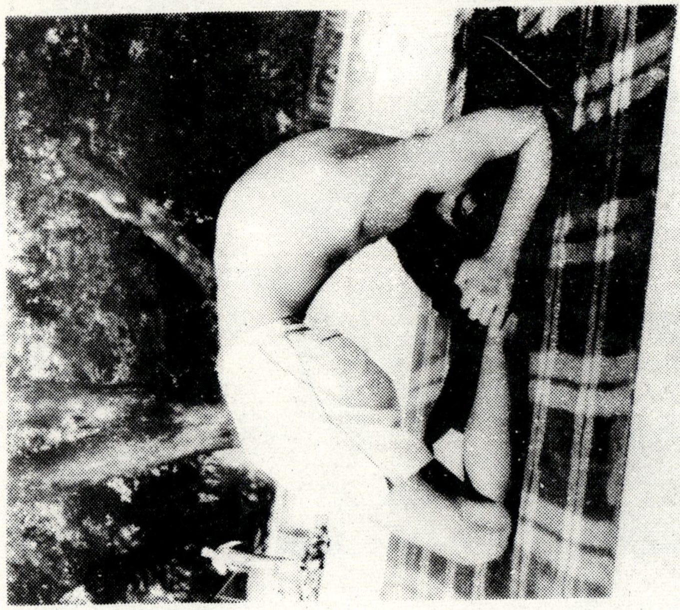

KAPOTASANA

TITTIBHASANA

MUDRAS AND BANDHAS

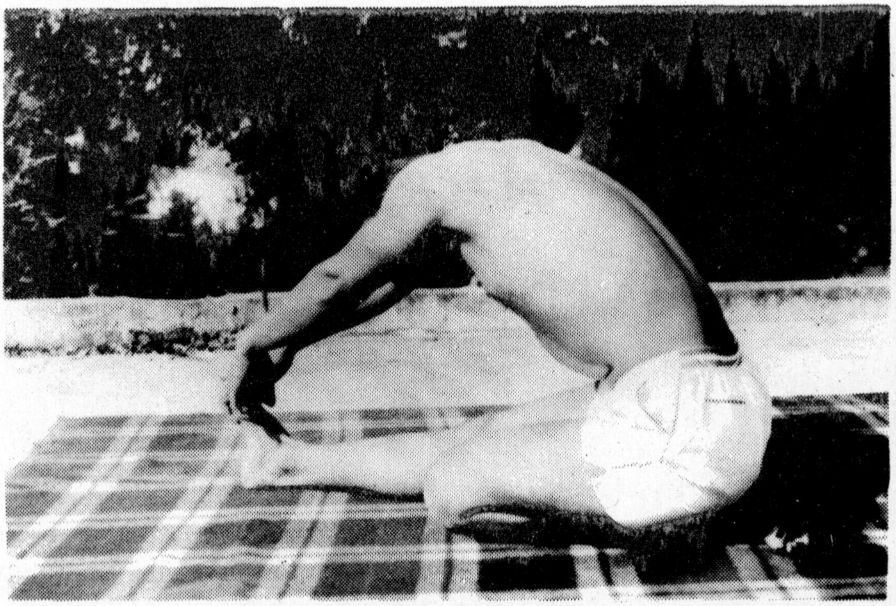

MAHA MUDRA (P. 75)

YOGA MUDRA (P. 76)

VIPARITAKARANI MUDRA (P. 77)

YONI MUDRA (P. 81)

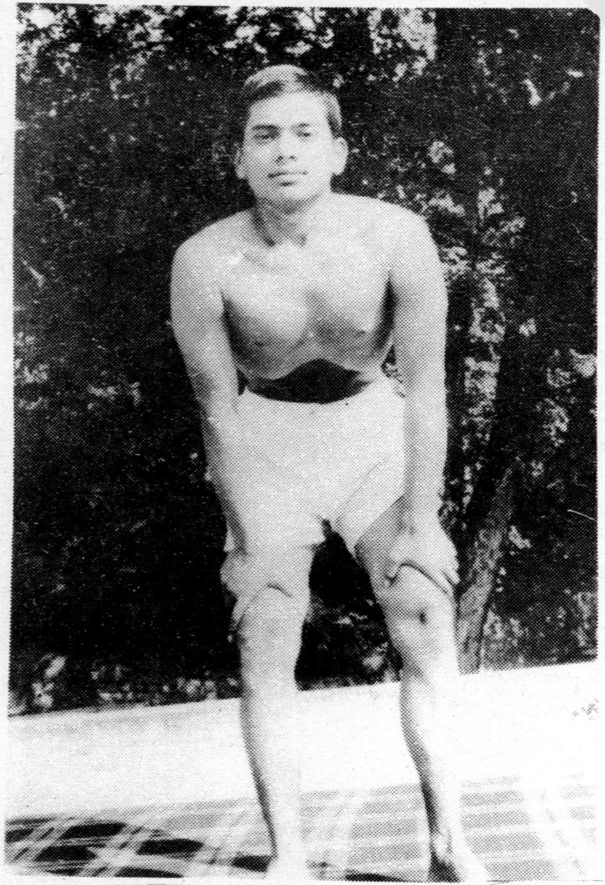

UDDIYANA BANDHA (P. 80) (*Front View*)

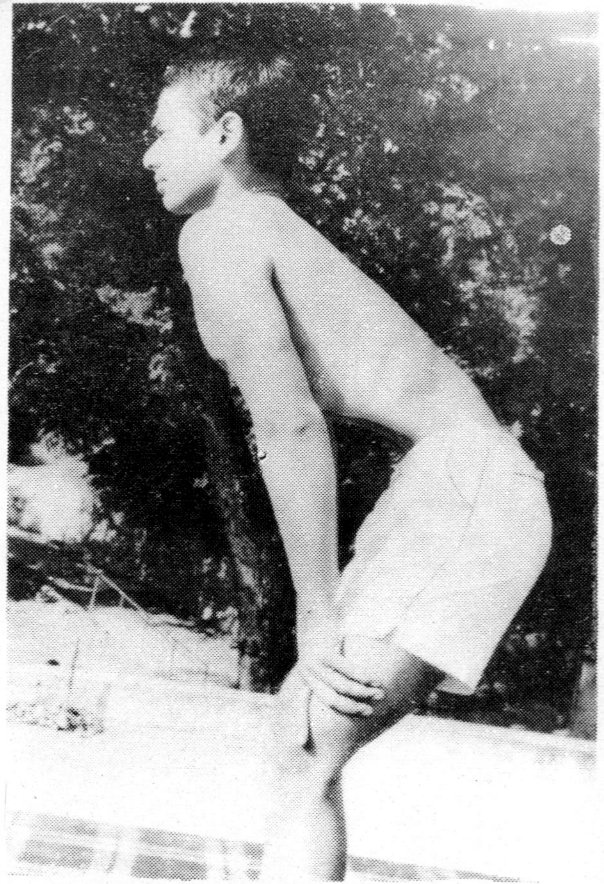

UDDIYANA BANDHA (*Side View*)

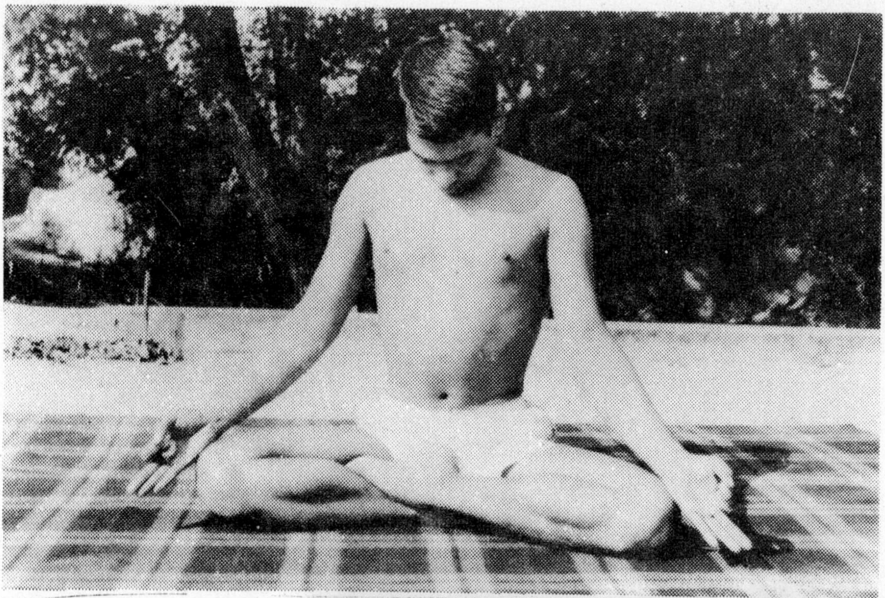

JALANDHARA
BANDHA

(P. 80)

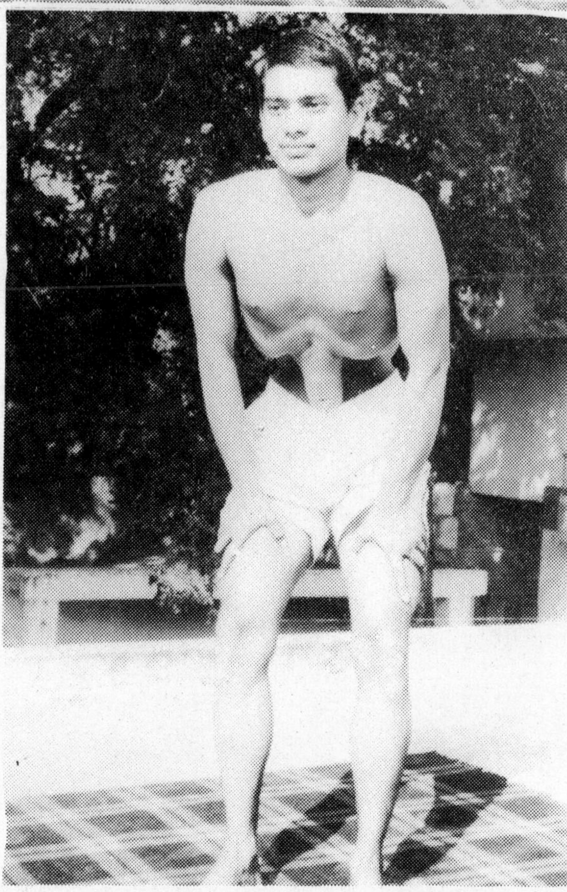

MADHYAMA NAULI

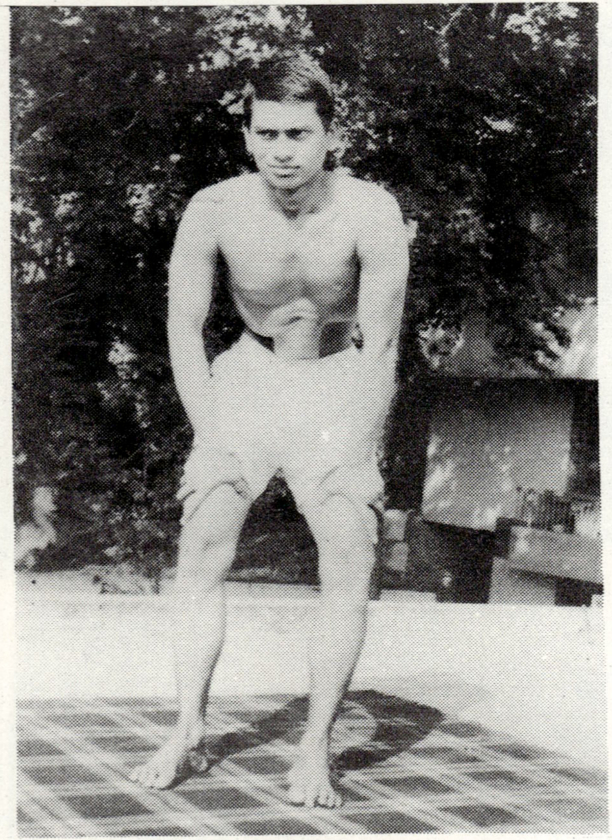
VAMA NAULI

DAKSHINA NAULI

PRANAYAMAS

SURYA BHEDA
(P. 84)

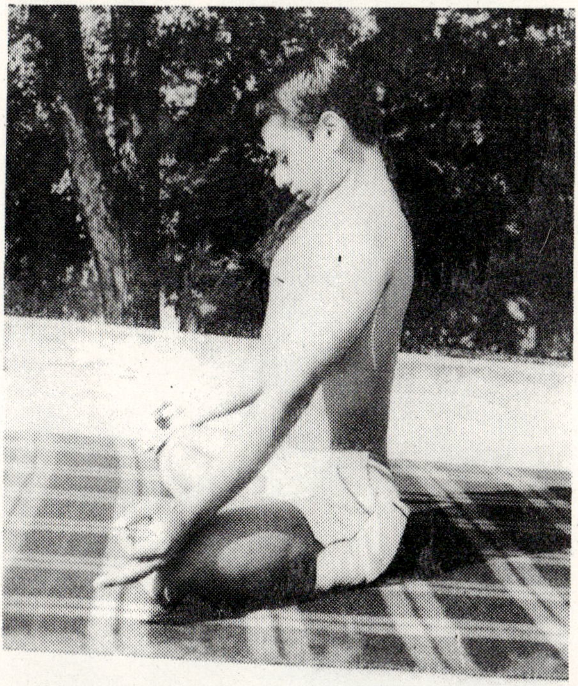

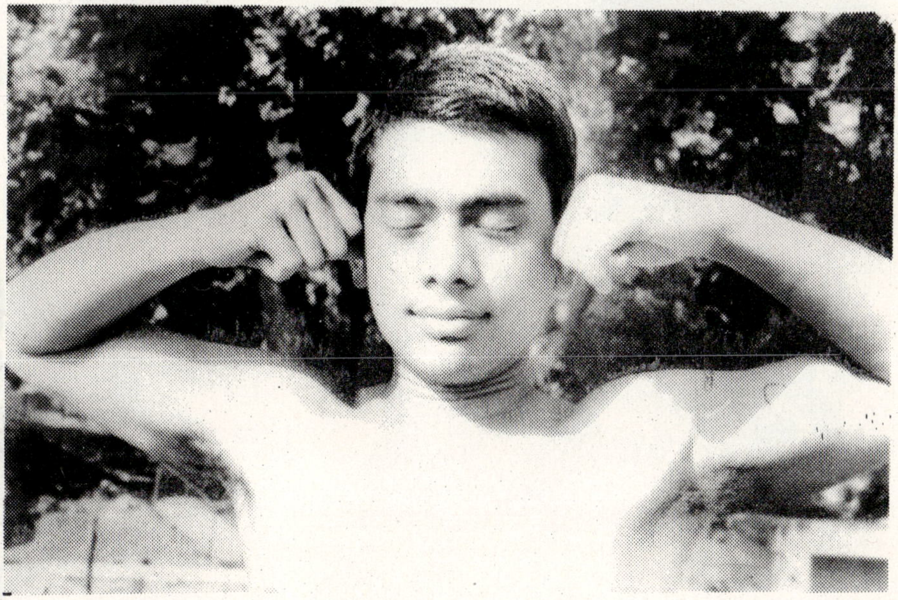

BHRAMARI (P. 88)

SITKARI (P. 85)

SITALI (P. 86)